Changing Islands

Eric Boagey

University Tutorial Press

Other books by Eric Boagey, published by University Tutorial Press, include:

English Workbook
Poetry Workbook
English for Me
Composition Choice
Starting Shakespeare

Published 1983

© E. J. Boagey 1983

ISBN 0 7231 0852 8

All rights reserved. No portion of this book may be reproduced by any process without written permission from the publishers.

Published by University Tutorial Press Ltd.
842 Yeovil Road, Slough SL1 4JQ

Printed by William Clowes (Beccles) Ltd, Beccles, Suffolk

A Note to Teachers

To say that there is something here for everyone would be unrealistic; but it could be claimed that there is something here for most. The themes and the poems themselves are deliberately wide-ranging, to suit those who want poems to tell exciting stories or express personal feelings or provoke an argument or simply to amuse. If there is a bias in the selection, it is towards the comprehensible, in order to counteract that strange conviction, clung to by so many schoolchildren, that poetry is 'difficult'.

Part of the difficulty arises out of the presentation. How should a poem be read in class? Silently by all? By the teacher, to do it justice? By a 'good' reader to let the others see how it can be done? Or by a 'poor' reader, to give him practice? The answer is not easy to find. The suggestions for reading the poems at the beginning of each section may go some way towards offering a solution by making the reading of poetry a prepared occasion, and particularly a shared one, akin to reading a play. If more take part, more are likely to respond to the meaning of the poem and poetry lessons could come alive.

Dare we ask what the purpose of it all is? Poetry can certainly be entertaining. Should it also make us think, become more aware of ourselves, of other people and the world we live in? This anthology will have failed in its purpose if it doesn't widen a few horizons, such as making its readers feel part, not only of a multi-cultural society, but also of a global one – hence the poems by West Indian writers, the ballads of the Australian bush, and the songs of the Cameroon. Even the poems in dialect may come as a surprise to those who thought that the language of poetry was confined to standard English.

Finally, a word about the questions at the end of each section. Aren't we killing poetry by making children stumble at these hurdles of comprehension? Well, they obviously weren't put there for that purpose. They can be answered orally and lead into a general discussion on the poems; but then not everyone in the class may take part. The written answer at least gives each individual a voice. The writing suggestions aim at fostering the creative imagination. In addition, throughout the land, year in, year out, students are writing essays on poetry for examination coursework. If the questions offer them guidance in this difficult area of critical writing, they will have fulfilled a need; and if the selection of poems gives pleasure as well as a sense of truth, it will have done what poetry is meant to do.

E.J.B.

Contents

Your Time of Life   1
   Lovely Morning   3
   Children   3
   What Has Happened to Lulu?   4
   Mother to Son   5
   Into Service   6
   The Punch Family   6
   Supermarket Tins   8
   Beauty Queen   9
   Teddy Boy   9
   The Reading Lesson   10
   A Difficult Child   12
   Latch-key Child   12
   And Not Tears   13
   Family Reunion   14

Changing Islands   19
   The Song of the Banana Man   21
   Ancestors   24
   The Fringe of the Sea   26
   The Emigrants   27
   Nock Nock Oo Nock E Nock   28
   Lucy's Letter   30
   Letter from England   31
   Thoughts on my Mother   32
   I Shall Return   33
   The Lament of the Banana Man   34
   From Lucy: new generation   35

Speaking Personally   39
   Gower Delivery   41
   Unfold Carefully   42
   The Watcher   42
   The Bicycle   44
   A Commonplace Day   45
   from *Man*   46
   How Many Miles   48
   Notes on the Way to the Block   49

Family Entertainment	50
Dinner Duty	51
Funambulist	52
Night Sorting in Victoria	52
A Song of the G.P.O.	54
Executive	54
Doctor Christmas	55

Bush Ballads   61

Jim Jones at Botany Bay	63
The Ballad of Jack Lefroy	64
The Drover's Dream	65
The Banks of the Condamine	66
The Death of Ben Hall	67
If Morgan Knew	70
The Mailman's Ride	71
A Bush Christening	76
Mulga Bill's Bicycle	77

Countrywide   83

Knees Up Mother Brown!	85
Boiled Beef and Carrots	87
A Hard Day's Night	88
The Bleed'n' Sparrer	89
Up Lunnon	90
The Lion and Albert	91
The Return of Albert	94
School Leaver	96
Omnibus Edition	97

Everything Lives   105

Movements	107
Hunting a Hare	107
Song of the Animal World	110
Elephant Song	111
Pig Farm Supreme	112
Milking Time	113
Praise of a Collie	114
The Early Purges	115
Hen Dying	116
Ella Mason and Her Eleven Cats	117
The Coral Polyp	118
The Spider	118
Turkeys	118
The Butterfly	118

Possible Futures 123
   Breakfast in Space 125
   Interferences ix 126
   Verdict 127
   We'll All Be Spacemen Before We Die 128
   Poem Written After Sighting an Unidentified Flying Object 128
   Jeux d'Enfants 130
   Shoot-out on Little Earth 132
   Progression of the Species 134
   The Basilisk 135
   Frankenstein 138
   The Gourds 139
   Last Message 140

Your Time of Life

As the title suggests, the poems in this first section are about the experiences of young people. They include the simple pleasure of fishing and an encounter between a boy and a girl in a supermarket. On a more serious note, there is a reaction to the news of a death, the pain and puzzlement of being caught between two parents who are on the verge of separation, and the problems of the 'difficult' child in the classroom. One poem looks back to the days when fourteen-year-old girls left home to go 'into service' in well-off families. But although the subject is young people, the point of view is occasionally that of the adult, as in *Mother to Son* and *Children*, where we see the anxieties and hopes of mothers as their children grow up.

In all these situations and relationships, you may see something that is true of *your* time of life.

Suggestions for reading the poems

Lovely Morning	Poet/narrator; first boy; man; foxy Paul.
Children	One reader throughout; or a separate reader for each of the nine *sentences* in the poem.
What Has Happened to Lulu?	One reader throughout; or a separate reader for each of the six verses.
Mother to Son	One reader, able to bring out the character and the Southern States accent of the mother.
Into Service	One reader.
The Punch Family	A reader for the quotation from Edmund Gosse. Poet/narrator; father.
Supermarket Tins	Boy; girl.
Beauty Queen	One reader.
Teddy Boy	One reader.
The Reading Lesson	Teacher; boy; neighbour.
A Difficult Child	One reader.
Latch-key Child	One reader.
And Not Tears	One reader.
Family Reunion	One reader for verses 1 and 3; a second reader for verse 2.

Lovely Morning

Foxy, freckle-faced suburban boys in denim
And lettered tee-shirts – QUEEN'S PARK RANGERS,
    SOUTHERN COMFORT,
TOO MUCH SEX MAKES YOUR EYES WEAK – fish the Surrey
    side from
Eel-Pie Island to the water tower at Brentford.

Their bikes whirr on the tow-paths – CHOPPER, HERCULES,
HUSTLER, drop-handlebarred with Continental gears
And dynamo and pennant. 'Got the *right* time please?'
Their self-adjusting floats, their patented spinners,

Their rods of fibreglass, their pink, disgusting things
In Tupperware bait-boxes ... 'It's ten to twelve.' 'Hey Paul,
Ten to twelve the man says.' A swan extends its wings
Heraldic on an oil-drum, and a bikini'd girl

Paddles a kayak delicately downstream.
'Lovely morning, Gorgeous!' shrills freckled, foxy Paul,
Hooking a fish as bright as aluminium.
The tautened nylon rasps and ratchets on the reel.

J. Whitworth

Children

Whether by careless accident
or careful plan
we are where they begin.

They grow in us
like germs or fictions
and we grow big with them.

Red, mewling strangers
they tear our thresholds
and immediately we love them.

When people say
they look like us
we smile and blush.

We listen for their cries
as if we felt their pain
and hunger deep in us

and hold them tightly
in our arms as if we'd found
a lost part of ourselves.

We want to give them
all the things we never had,
to make it up to them

for all the times
when we were hurt or sad,
to start again and put right

our mistakes in them,
to run in front of them
with warning flags.

We who've failed to be
the authors of our lives
write theirs.

We make them heroes,
stars whose happy endings
will scatter light in ours.

We feed them with our dreams
then wait and watch
like gardeners for flowers.

Vicki Feaver

What Has Happened to Lulu?

What has happened to Lulu, mother?
  What has happened to Lu?
There's nothing in her bed but an old rag doll
  And by its side a shoe.

Why is her window wide, mother,
  The curtain flapping free,
And only a circle on the dusty shelf
  Where her money-box used to be?

Why do you turn your head, mother,
  And why do the tear-drops fall?
And why do you crumple that note on the fire
  And say it is nothing at all?

I woke to voices late last night,
  I heard an engine roar.
Why do you tell me the things I heard
  Were a dream and nothing more?

I heard somebody cry, mother,
  In anger or in pain,
But now I ask you why, mother,
  You say it was a gust of rain.

Why do you wander about as though
  You don't know what to do?
What has happened to Lulu, mother?
  What has happened to Lu?   *Charles Causley*

Mother to Son

Well, son, I'll tell you:
Life for me ain't been no crystal stair.
It's had tacks in it,
And splinters,
And boards torn up,
And places with no carpet on the floor –
Bare.
But all the time
I'se been a-climbin' on,
And reachin' landin's,
And turnin' corners,
And sometimes goin' in the dark
Where there ain't been no light.
So, boy, don't you turn back.
Don't you set down on the steps
'Cause you finds it's kinder hard.
Don't you fall now
For I'se still goin', honey,
I'se still climbin',
And life for me ain't been no crystal stair.   *Langston Hughes*

Into Service

Two trunks holding –
Black stockings, strong shoes,
Newspaper gifts of 'Little Women',
Liberty bodices, big bloomers,
Afternoon dresses,
Caps and aprons,
Two of everything.
Lonely and frightened,
Guzzled by big houses
These fourteen-year-old girls
Left mam and dad,
Childhood and home,
For ten bob a week bondage,
Drudgery of work-long days
For immature bodies.
Shed cold, attic tears.
Red-raw hands sent money home.
But, Christ, they were tough,
Indomitable,
Made the best of it.
Tassels from chairs trimmed their dresses.
Medicine bottles of whisky smuggled out.
Tablets of soap slipped into bloomers.
Forty years on
Turkish towels rub their families dry.
A cheeky evening out.
A slight redress of the balance.
A fifth column
Shifting society.

Helen Hudgell

The Punch Family

'I was much affected by the internal troubles of the Punch family. I thought that with a little more tact on the part of Mrs Punch and some restraint held over a temper, naturally violent, by Mr Punch, a great deal of this sad misunderstanding might have been prevented.'

(Edmund Gosse: *Father and Son*)

He was always alone in this:
each holiday, with seaside friends
who weren't his friends, he gazed
at a high tent's awful hole
and shuddered. Something amiss,
unnameable, a huge stick
pummelling his shapeless soul
like pastry. Even the jolly stripes
reminded him of blood. Amazed,
not as a child is by some party trick,
he learned from squeaking archetypes
the terror on which life depends.

And later, back at the grim hotel
which never let him out of sight
but set a righteous face against the sea
in red-bricked anger, echoes
put on flesh; 'Your mother isn't well . . .
this place . . . the air . . .' His father's voice
was hard like making deals. 'She chose
to rest a little on her own this afternoon.
I had a word with them. They sent up tea.
I don't know why we come here. It's *her* choice.'
Something was still unnameable but soon
that show, too, finished for the night.

At breakfast, nothing made sense.
Once more the same pain
shuddered across the table as they thrust
their glumness at each other. Why?
What huge stick in the silence
hung above them? When would it hammer down
and end this? When would she cry
or he be gone forever?
                    So, each holiday
each morning, always, one small boy must
leave them alone in this, a fixed frown
souring his heart, and, friendless, go and play
with friends, and in the evening come again.

John Mole

Supermarket Tins

There were rows of coca cola
on the supermarket stand,
shimmering under white light,
reflecting silver and red.
And perfectly between two tins
(consciously apart)
was framed her arresting face
so dramatically decorated.
Blonded hair parted with a razorsharp edge,
freckles on a structured nose cast along a classic line.
'I'll see you again,'
I heard myself say,
when really I want to feel,
to touch, smell, sense and explorate
the mind behind
the body contours, built of clay.
'I feel I know you,'
she replied
standing by the timeless, cylindered tins.
Her body patterns silently dissolved
as this becalmed, oasis moment slid away
and tins in supermarkets became just
supermarket tins.

Nicholas Nuttall

Beauty Queen

I remember, I remember,
The year I won the prize,
The little judges peeping at
My bosom and my thighs;
I could not wear a stitch too few,
To show my winning form,
But now they've sent me back to school
To gym-slips and the dorm!

I remember, I remember,
The telly and the stage
Bombarding me with offers till
They heard about my age;
I've got to pass the G.C.E. –
It fills me full of spleen
To think I've got more subjects now
Than when I was a Queen.

Audrey L. Laski

Teddy Boy

(To Gloria, from Jail)

Wannit smashin', wannit smashin',
the dump where I hung out;
the Old Man use ter come 'ome cut
and knock me Mum about;
and last night's empties by the stairs
as up ter kip I goes,
and the tin trunk on the landin'
where I put me Teddy clothes.

Wannit smashin', wannit smashin',
the Palais and the Dive.
Remember when I done that bloke
fer askin' yer to jive?
And The Bug 'ouse every uvver night,
and fags and Dogs and beer.
I tell yer, I'm gonna Go The Lot
when I get out of 'ere.

Tommy the Duffle

The Reading Lesson

Fourteen years old, learning the alphabet,
He finds letters harder to catch than hares
Without a greyhound. Can't I give him a dog
To track them down, or put them in a cage?
He's caught in a trap, until I let him go,
Pinioned by 'Don't you want to learn to read?'
'I'll be the same man whatever I do.'

He looks at a page as a mule balks at a gap
From which a goat may hobble out and bleat.
His eyes jink from a sentence like flushed snipe
Escaping shot. A sharp word, and he'll mooch
Back to his piebald mare and bantam cock.
Our purpose is as tricky to retrieve
As mercury from a smashed thermometer.

'I'll not read any more.' Should I give up?
His hands, long-fingered as a Celtic scribe's,
Will grow callous, gathering sticks or scrap;
Exploring pockets of the horny drunk
Loiterers at the fairs, giving them lice.
A neighbour chuckles. 'You can never tame
The wild-duck: when his wings grow, he'll fly off.'

If books resembled roads, he'd quickly read:
But they're small farms to him, fenced by the page,
Ploughed into lines, with letters drilled like oats:
A field of tasks he'll always be outside.
If words were bank-notes, he would filch a wad;
If they were pheasants, they'd be in his pot
For breakfast, or if wrens he'd make them king.

Richard Murphy

A Difficult Child

More proficient than a ventriloquist,
he imitates birdcalls with a shut mouth;
with a conjurer's deftness, he can throw
balls of paper across the class without
moving his hands from the desk. He can spit
bubble-gum so high into the air that
it sticks to the ceiling. Whatever he
does, demands attention. Once he even
lit a cigarette, took a puff, and stubbed
it out in a sudden mime so swiftly
executed that he didn't seem to move
at all, and the whole class applauded him.
Chewing paper, he rolls it on his tongue
and shoots it right into the teacher's ear.
Twelve years ago when chocolates were
rationed and flowers expensive, a young
man gave a girl this bastard. The teacher
wonders what use punishment would be for
one who has never known anything else.

Zulfikar Ghose

Latch-key Child

I found him
sitting in the cold dark room
watching television
and stuffing himself with sweets.

'Why didn't you,' I asked,
'turn the light and fire on?'
He didn't answer.
Just fingered his cap, embarrassed.

And then I remembered
how I'd once waited in the dark –
thinking that if I kept still
so would the shadow by the window.

Vicki Feaver

And Not Tears

Years backward when a young girl who had lost
A parent, set out on a washing day
To do what she could which was not much,

The old woman who helped came along
A poor fat creature of featureless face,
And standing on the scullery's wet floor

Amidst the segregated heaps there waiting
Burst suddenly into tears because her man had died
And I, a young girl, could only see

The red distorted face struggling with words
And laughter broke in spasms in my body,
It was all I could do to conceal it,

Run out of the way, holding my breath,
Shaking with this high laughter that I
Had to let escape without her knowledge.

Afterwards I was ashamed, for I had pity
For her as for my own lonely plight
(And my father ready to marry again

For the third time). Also beside shame
Was something else, fear. That her poor knotted face
Should make me shake with laughter and not tears.

Madge Hales

Family Reunion

Outside in the street I hear
A car door slam; voices coming near;
Incoherent scraps of talk
And high heels clicking up the walk;
The doorbell rends the noonday heat
With copper claws;
A second's pause.
  The dull drums of my pulses beat
Against a silence wearing thin.
The door now opens from within.
Oh, hear the clash of people meeting –
The laughter and the screams of greeting:

Fat always, and out of breath,
A greasy smack on every cheek
From Aunt Elizabeth;
There, that's the pink, pleased squeak
Of Cousin Jane, our spinster with
The faded eyes
And hands like nervous butterflies;
While rough as splintered wood
  Across them all
Rasps the jarring baritone of Uncle Paul:
The youngest nephew gives a fretful whine
And drools at the reception line.

Like a diver on a lofty spar of land
Atop the flight of stairs I stand.
A whirlpool leers at me,
Absorbent as a sponge;
I cast off my identity
And make the fatal plunge.

Sylvia Plath

Some questions on the poems

Children

1. Let us say you were a child of the mother in the poem. Can you express what your feelings would be towards her?

2. You will notice that the mother in the poem shows great love for her children, but she is also critical of herself. What exactly does she accuse herself of?

3. Can you write a poem or a paragraph describing a child's relationship with its parents or with other adults? What feelings link them? What feelings separate them?

What Has Happened to Lulu?

4. The fascination of the poem is in the unanswered questions, but there are details which give us clues as to what has happened to Lulu. From these, can you reconstruct the events of the night and write about them in the form of a short story?

Looking more closely at *The Punch Family*

5.
   a) It seems contradictory, but can you suggest a meaning for the expression 'friends who weren't his friends'?
   b) What was the boy watching in the tent's 'awful hole'?
   c) Why didn't he seem to enjoy what he was watching?
   d) What sort of hotel do you think could be described as having 'a righteous face'?
   e) Which words in the poem suggest that the boy couldn't quite explain to himself what was wrong between his parents?
   f) Why is the poem called *The Punch Family*?
   g) With whom do you think the poet's sympathies lie?
   h) What are *your* feelings about the situation it describes?

The Reading Lesson

6. What kind of life did the boy lead when he wasn't at school? From the details that are given in the poem, can you piece together a picture of what he did and write it up in a short paragraph?

7   Richard Murphy uses some very effective comparisons in the poem to bring out the boy's reading difficulties. For instance: 'He finds letters harder to catch than hares without a greyhound'. Jot down any others that you think are particularly good.

8   The poet-teacher asks: 'Should I give up?' What do you think? Ought he to persist in trying to teach the boy to read or not? What are the arguments for and against?

The characters

These poems present young people in various situations – happy, romantic, tragic, painful, amusing, awkward.

Which characters did you simply like best? Which had you some sympathy for? Which seemed to be presented in a 'true life' situation? Which meant very little to you?

In answering these questions, give reasons for your choices by referring to the details of the poems themselves.

Writing a poem

Some of the poems might help you to write poetry yourself – particularly those that don't rhyme and are written in a conversational style. Here are some suggestions:

1   Describe a morning's (or afternoon's) enjoyment during a holiday or at the week-end. What did you do? Who was with you? What amusing or exciting things happened?

2   *Into Service* looks back at the time when young people of your age went out to work. Can you write a poem from the point of view of a person in the 21st century who looks back at the young people of today and describes how they lived?

3 *Beauty Queen* and *Teddy Boy* are comic imitations of a sentimental Victorian poem that begins:

> 'I remember, I remember,
> The house where I was born,
> The little window where the sun
> Came peeping in at morn.'

Try writing your own version of this poem in which you recollect scenes and incidents from your childhood. You may find it easier to write in short lines without rhyme.

4 Write about an imaginary character in school. Show what attitude he or she has towards lessons and try to make your reader understand – as Zulfikar Ghose and Richard Murphy do – the reasons for your character's behaviour.

5 What is a 'family reunion' like in your house? Briefly describe some of your relatives and express what you yourself feel when they arrive for a family get-together.

Changing Islands

That Britain is now a multi-racial society is due in part to the migration of peoples over the past few decades from the islands of the Caribbean to these northern isles. The changes in climate, culture and social attitude the emigrants encountered brought experiences and emotions which found expression in a rich body of West Indian poetry, some of which is included in this section.

The poems follow the cycle from life in the Caribbean, through emigration and readjustment to a new environment in Britain. We start off with a song about the life of a 'banana man' in the Caribbean and end with a letter from James Berry's wonderful character, Lucy, whose children represent the new generation, their roots already established in the country of their birth.

Some of the poems are in the form of monologues, spoken by characters in their own style of speech; others are direct expressions of the poet's own feelings. Together they form a vivid portrait, humorous as well as moving, of the West Indian experience in both the Caribbean and Britain.

Suggestions for reading the poems

The Song of the Banana Man	A separate reader for each of the seven stanzas (including the refrains); or seven additional readers for the refrains; or a single reader for all the refrains.
Ancestors	A separate reader for each of the three parts of the poem.
The Fringe of the Sea	A new reader to take over after each full-stop, which means five readers for verses: 1, 2–3, 4–6, 7–8, 9.
The Emigrants	Five readers for verses: 1, 2, 3, 4, 5–6.
Nock Nock Oo Nock E Nock	Two readers – good ones who are prepared to tackle the dialect. Some practice time should be allowed.
Lucy's Letter	A separate reader for each of the five verses.
Letter from England	One reader.
Thoughts on my Mother	One reader.
I Shall Return	One reader.
The Lament of the Banana Man	Three readers for verses: 1–3, 4–5, 6–7.
From Lucy: new generation	Two readers for verses: 1–3, 4–6.

The Song of the Banana Man

Touris', white man, wipin' his face,
Met me in Golden Grove market place.
He looked at me ol' clothes brown wid stain,
An' soaked right through wid de Portlan' rain.
He cas' his eye, turn' up his nose;
He says, 'You're a beggar man, I suppose?'
He says, 'Boy, get some occupation;
Be of some value to your nation.'

I said, 'By God an' dis big right han',
You mus' recognize a banana man.

'Up in de hills, where de streams are cool,
An' mullet an' janga swim in de pool,
I have ten acres of mountain side,
An' a dainty-foot donkey dat I ride,
Four Gros Michel, an' four Lacatan,
Some coconut trees, an' some hills of yam,
An' I pasture on dat very same lan'
Five she-goats an' a big black ram;

'Dat, by God an' dis big right han',
Is de property of a banana man.

'I leave me yard early-mornin' time
An' set me foot to de mountain climb;
I ben' me back to de hot-sun toil,
An' me cutlass rings on de stony soil,
Ploughin' an' weedin', diggin' an' plantin',
Till Massa Sun drop back o' John Crow mountain,
Den home again in cool evenin' time,
Perhaps whistlin' dis likkle rhyme:

(SUNG) 'Praise God an' me big right han',
I will live an' die a banana man.

'Banana day is me special day;
I cut me stems an' I'm on me way;
Load up de donkey, leave de lan',
Head down de hill to banana stan';
When de truck comes roun', I take a ride
All de way down to de harbour side.
Dat is de night, when you, touris' man,
Would change you' place wid a banana man.

'Yes, by God an' me big right han',
I will live an' die a banana man.

'De bay is calm, an' de moon is bright;
De hills look black for de sky is light;
Down at de docks is an English ship,
Restin' after her ocean trip,
While on de pier is a monstrous hustle,
Tallymen, carriers, all in a bustle,
Wid stems on deir heads in a long black snake,
Some singin' de songs dat banana men make:

'Like, (SUNG) 'Praise God an' me big right han',
I will live an' die a banana man.

'Den de payment comes, an' we have some fun,
Me, Zekiel, Breda an' Duppy Son.
Down at de bar near United Wharf,
We knock back a white rum, bus' a laugh,
Fill de empty bag for further toil
Wid saltfish, breadfruit, coconut oil,
Den head back home to me yard to sleep
A proper sleep dat is long an' deep.

'Yes, by God an' me big right han',
I will live an' die a banana man.

'So when you see dese ol' clothes brown wid stain,
An' soaked right through wid de Portlan' rain,
Don't cas' you' eye or turn you' nose,
Don't judge a man by his patchy clothes;
I'm a strong man, a proud man, an' I'm free,
Free as dese mountains, free as dis sea;
I know m'self, an' I know me ways,
An' will sing wid pride to de end o' me days:

(SUNG) 'Praise God an' me big right han',
I will live an' die a banana man.'

Evan Jones

Ancestors

1
Every Friday morning my grandfather
left his farm of canefields, chickens, cows,
and rattled in his trap down to the harbour town
to sell his meat. He was a butcher.
Six-foot-three and very neat: high collar,
winged, a grey cravat, a waistcoat, watch-
chain just above the belt, thin narrow-
bottomed trousers, and the shoes his wife
would polish every night. He drove the trap
himself: slap of the leather reins
along the horse's back and he'd be off
with a top-hearted homburg on his head:
black English country gentleman.

Now he is dead. The meat shop burned,
his property divided. A doctor bought
the horse. His mad alsatians killed it.
The wooden trap was chipped and chopped
by friends and neighbours and used to stop-
gap fences and for firewood. One yellow
wheel was rolled across the former cowpen gate.
Only his hat is left. I 'borrowed' it.
I used to try it on and hear the night wind
man go battering through the canes, cocks waking up and thinking
it was dawn throughout the clinking country night.
Great caterpillar tractors clatter down
the broken highway now; a diesel engine grunts
where pigs once hunted garbage.
A thin asthmatic cow shares the untrashed garage.

2
All that I can remember of his wife,
my father's mother, is that she sang us songs
('Great Tom Is Cast' was one), that frightened me.
And she would go chug-chugging with a jar
of milk until its white pap turned to yellow
butter. And in the basket underneath the stairs
she kept the polish for grandfather's shoes.

All that I have of her is voices:
laughing me out of fear because a crappaud
jumped and splashed the dark where I was huddled
in the galvanized tin bath; telling us stories
round her fat white lamp. It was her Queen
Victoria lamp, she said; although the stamp
read Ever Ready. And in the night, I listened to her singing
in a Vicks and Vapour Rub-like voice what you would call the
  blues

3
Come-a look
come-a look
see wha' happen

come-a look
come-a look
see wha' happen

Sookey dead
Sookey dead
Sookey dead-o

Sookey dead
Sookey dead
Sookey dead-o.

Him a-wuk
him a-wuk
till 'e bleed-o

him a-wuk
him a-wuk
till 'e bleed-o

Sookey dead
Sookey dead
Sookey dead-o

Sookey dead
Sookey dead
Sookey dead-o . . .

Edward Brathwaite

The Fringe of the Sea

We do not like to awaken
far from the fringe of the sea,
we who live upon small islands.

We like to rise up early,
quick in the agile mornings
and walk out only little distances
to look down at the water,

to know it is swaying near to us
with songs, and tides, and endless boatways,
and undulate patterns and moods.

We want to be able to saunter beside it
slowpaced in burning sunlight,
barearmed, barefoot, bareheaded,

and to stoop down by the shallows
sifting the random water
between assaying fingers
like farmers do with soil,

and to think of turquoise mackerel
turning with consummate grace,
sleek and decorous
and elegant in high blue chambers.

We want to be able to walk out into it,
to work in it,
dive and swim and play in it,

to row and sail
and pilot over its sandless highways,
and to hear
its call and murmurs wherever we may be.

All who have lived upon small islands
want to sleep and awaken
close to the fringe of the sea.

A. L. Hendriks

The Emigrants

So you have seen them
with their cardboard grips,
felt hats, rain-
cloaks, the women
with their plain
or purple-tinted
coats hiding their fatten-
ed hips.

These are The Emigrants.
On sea-port quays
at air-ports
anywhere where there is ship
or train, swift
motor car, or jet
to travel faster than the breeze
you see them gathered:
passports stamped
their travel papers wrapped
in old disused news-
papers: lining their patient queues.

Where to?
They do not know.
Canada, the Panama
Canal, the Miss-
issippi painfields, Florida?
Or on to dock
at hissing smoke locked
Glasgow?

Why do they go?
They do not know.
Seeking a job
they settle for the very best
the agent has to offer:
jabbing a neighbour
out of work for four bob
less a week.

What do they hope for
what find there
these New World mariners
Columbus coursing kaffirs?

What Cathay shores
for them are gleaming golden
what magic keys they carry to unlock
what gold endragoned doors?

Edward Brathwaite

Enoch Powell, M.P., wants the government to encourage black immigrants to return to their countries of origin.

Nock Nock Oo Nock E Nock

Me was fas asleep in me bed
wen a nok come pun me door;
bright and early, fore day morning
before dawn bruk.
Nock nock – nock nock,
badoombadoom nock nock
badoombadoom nock nock
badoombadoom nock badoom nock
who dat; a who dat nock?
E nock.
Is what ya mean e nock?
You wha nock.
No, no, no e nock
You nock.
No no e nock,
E nock gwine sen ya back.

Back ta weh?
Back ta wha?
Back ta weh ya come from.
Why him gwine do dat?
Wha me da?
Ya na da natin, but him sey,
sen dem back,
sen dem darkies back,
sa ya hav a ga.
Wha me wan a no is,
'f me na da natin
why him sen me back?
Him sey ya too many
ya polute de place.
Me na polute natin.
Him sey ya na wok,
ya na tek ya opportunity.
Sa ya hav ta ga back,
to little England
to Trafalgar Square and Lord Horatio Nelson.
Back to Bimsha?
Weh de people dem cook wid salt
and de food nice?
It nice nice ya no.
Da breadfruit, cassava
sweet potato, pumpkin,
eddoes and yam
dem mek me mout water
and de sugar-cane,
wid de licker straight from the factory,
or de sea-egg and cat-fish and 'ting,
and don't talk 'bout de flying fish,
or de fruit tree.
Why me na see guava heh,
nor mammy apple, starch apple,
sour-sop, papu, golden apple,
and all dom'ting;
Coconut water wid mont-gay rum.
Is he gwine sen me back ta all dat
eh eh! A mus ee really do like like Bear Rabbit
is sa it ga? Me glad ya nock – e nock.

Jimi Rand

Lucy's Letter

Things harness me here. I long
for we labrish bad. Doors
not fixed open here.
No Leela either. No Cousin
Lil, Miss Lottie or Bro'-Uncle.
Dayclean doesn' have cockcrowin'.
Midmornin' doesn' bring
Cousin-Maa with her naseberry tray.
Afternoon doesn' give a ragged
Manwell, strung with fish
like bright leaves. Seven days
play same note in London, chile.
But Leela, money-rustle regular.

Mi dear, I don' laugh now,
not'n' like we thunder claps
in darkness on verandah.
I turned a battery hen
in 'lectric light, day an' night.
No mood can touch one
mango season back at Yard.
At least though I did start
evening school once.
An' doctors free, chile.

London isn' like we
village dirt road, you know
Leela: it a parish
of a pasture-lan' what
grown crisscross streets,
an' they lie down to my door.
But I lock myself in.
I carry keys everywhere.
Life here's no open summer,
girl. But Sat'day mornin' don'
find mi han' dry, don' find my face
a heavy cloud over the man.

An' though he still have
a weekend mind for bat 'n' ball
he wash a dirty dish now, mi dear.
It sweet him I on the Pill.
We get money for holidays.
But there's no sun-hot
to enjoy cool breeze.

Leela, I really a sponge
you know, for traffic noise,
for work noise, for halfway
intentions, for halfway smiles,
for clockwatchin' an' col' weather.
I hope you don't think I gone
too fat when we meet.
I booked up to come an' soak
the children in daylight.

James Berry

Letter from England

In autumn when the air is crisp
And dusk encroaches on the tea-time sky,
Well wrapped in scarves I sometimes take a stroll
And see the daylight fade.
The time is quite unlike that quarter-hour
When darkness drops so suddenly at home:
Here there's no fireball sunset gaily warm
That laughs a promise of the day's return,
Only the calm good manners of a soft farewell
And day has passed to evening.

Mervyn Morris

Thoughts on my Mother

Bare trees turn the mind
to palm leaves a-rattle round
an open house with shadows wild
about a boy stretching sinews
in the stings and wash
of your voice your hands your eyes

Your oiled hand makes a cross
on my belly, and all
pain goes

Caretaker of my beginnings your echoes
pull me in and out from where many
bare feet slap earth floor,
secure, under the thatch cured in smoke
old as granpuppa, your domain
wattled in, with smells mixed with
ginger, nutmeg and pimento berries
and old sweat of donkey padding

And your pestle a-crush woodfired
coffeebeans and cocoabeans
with cinnamon, and corn and cassava,
and no food is ever the same
after your salted pepper spice-up
from a sapling table

December is stuck in gardens
and bed blankets here
but red hibiscus opens up
the playmates' wood-and-straw
place, and the song in your hair
like your patience I could
never have, with your luxury
iced water in a calabash

Woman
you hang no accomplishments:
it's one late gold ring a-flash
your only jewel, yet eight people's
habits and clothes-fabric were
like a map in your palm

Frost winds in England try
to skin me white: you are
warm, your face
wet in sweat, black in sunlight
as you dig, chop or stitch,
with feet bare like
the scorpions and centipedes,
that I may let go my tasselled roots
the sun pulls upward.

James Berry

I Shall Return

I shall return again, I shall return
To laugh and love and watch with wonder-eyes
At golden noon the forest fires burn,
Wafting their blue-black smoke to sapphire skies.
I shall return to loiter by the streams
That bathe the brown blades of the bending grasses,
And realize once more my thousand dreams
Of waters surging down the mountain passes.
I shall return to hear the fiddle and fife
Of village dances, dear delicious tunes
That stir the hidden depths of native life,
Stray melodies of dim-remembered runes.
I shall return. I shall return again
To ease my mind of long, long years of pain.

Claude McKay

The Lament of the Banana Man

Gal, I'm tellin' you, I'm tired fo' true,
Tired of Englan', tired o' you.
But I can't go back to Jamaica now ...

I'm here in Englan', I'm drawin' pay,
I go to de underground every day –
Eight hours is all, half-hour fo' lunch,
M' uniform's free, an' m' ticket punch –
Punchin' tickets not hard to do,
When I'm tired o' punchin', I let dem through.

I get a paid holiday once a year.
Ol' age an' sickness can't touch me here.

I have a room of m' own, an' a iron bed,
Dunlopillo under m' head,
A Morphy-Richards to warm de air,
A formica table, an easy chair.
I have summer clothes, an' winter clothes,
An' paper kerchiefs to blow m' nose.

My yoke is easy, my burden is light,
I know a place I can go to, any night.
Dis place Englan'! I'm not complainin',
If it col', it col', if it rainin', it rainin'.
I don't min' if it's mostly night,
Dere's always inside, or de sodium light.

I don't min' white people starin' at me,
Dey don' want me here? Don't is deir country?
You won' catch me bawlin' any homesick tears,
If I don' see Jamaica for a t'ousan' years!

... Gal, I'm tellin' you, I'm tired fo' true,
Tired of Englan', tired o' you,
I can't go back to Jamaica now –
But I'd want to die there, anyhow.

Evan Jones

From Lucy: new generation

Yes, Leela, full teenagers now,
Tony an' Sharon. An' free at school
to work or squander time.
Thank God they hol' their own.
They body blemish free
an' you'd think they have no fear.

I did want them know the Bible,
know Shakespeare. Mi dear, they
pity me. They say I still missing
links, I still don' understan'
world without black gods isn'
in worlds without end. The Buddha,
Mohammed, Jah, all
know the way they say.

They different breed mi dear.
The heads are Afro style.
They wear patches on the bum
to show they side with the poor.

Westindies is jus' a place parents
born: Bob Marley's their only thought
in it. 'Beat' sounds hypnotise them.
Beat makers give them religion.

An' it's their joke I teachin'
mi English neighbour Westindian Talk.
They eat'n' curry-an'-rice now
I say, they need little
Westindies Talk to season it.
They laugh at me an' say I funny.

Mi dear, we all
lookin', lookin', lookin'.
Remember, 'One han' washes the other'.

James Berry

Explanations

The Song of the Banana Man

mullet, janga	species of fish
Gros Michel, Lacatan	varieties of banana trees
Massa Sun	Mister Sun

Ancestors

crappaud	toad

The Emigrants

grips	suitcases
Kaffirs	South Africans of Bantu race
Cathay	China

Nock Nock Oo Nock E Nock

gwine	going to
wha me da?	what me done?
natin	nothing
little England	a local name for Barbados
Trafalgar Square	a square in Bridgetown, Barbados, where there is a statue of Lord Nelson
Bimsha	Barbados
cassava, eddoes	tropical root vegetables
guava, mammy apple, starch apple, sour-sop, papu, golden apple	tropical fruits

Lucy's Letter

labrish	talk, gossip
naseberry tray	seller's tray of naseberries: soft, sweet Caribbean fruits

Thoughts on my Mother

red hibiscus	a shrubby, flowering plant
calabash	a gourd used as a container

Some questions on the poems

1. We get a strong impression of West Indian characters from the poems. Which three did you find most interesting? Can you describe them and, by using quotations, explain how the poet has been able to make us feel that they were real people?

2. Perhaps these poems have given you a glimpse of a way of life you knew nothing about before you read them. If so, look through them again, then make some notes under the general heading I DIDN'T KNOW THAT ... describing what you have learnt about West Indian life and people.

3. Many of these poems are written in a West Indian dialect and contain expressions that are probably new to you, like the Banana Man's 'By God an' dis big right han'' or Lucy's 'Dayclean doesn' have cock-crowin''. Can you find some more examples of the richness and originality of West Indian speech?

4. Look again at the poems which are written from the point of view of the West Indian immigrant – *Nock Nock Oo Nock E Nock*, *Lucy's Letter* and *The Lament of the Banana Man*, for instance. What did the newcomers find satisfying about their life in England? What did they dislike? What did they miss most?

5. Some poems are written out of respect and admiration for a person whom the poet knew as a child. What did Edward Brathwaite admire in his grandfather and grandmother? For what qualities does James Berry remember his mother?

Looking more closely at the Banana Man poems

The Song of the Banana Man

6. a) Why does the tourist think the Banana Man is a beggar?
   b) The Banana Man obviously takes a pride and a delight in his property and his work. What exactly does he own? What kind of work does he do on his land?
   c) What gives us the impression that he is a happy man?

d) Write a short description of what he does on his 'special day'.
e) Which line in the last verse of the poem seems to sum up the Banana Man's character?

7
The Lament of the Banana Man
a) Why do you think this poem is called a 'lament' whereas the other is called a 'song'?
b) If you compare the two poems, which life seems to be the better one for the Banana Man himself – life in Jamaica or in England? Why?

Your own writing

What have you learnt about the composition of poetry from these poems? Perhaps that it is possible to write in a relaxed, conversational way and still produce the rhythms and imaginative phrasing that we think of as being typical of poetry.

Try writing a poem yourself, based on your own style of speech or that of a character you create, expressing thoughts on a subject of your own choosing, or on one of the following:
My Generation
I wish that . . .
Memories.

Speaking Personally

Here is a gallery of self-portraits – that is, poems in which a character speaks directly to the reader and reveals something of his or her own nature. Some speakers are obviously the poets themselves, like the Girl, the Teacher and the Cyclist; other speakers have been invented by the poet in order to show us what is going on in the character's mind. Occasionally the poets have tricks up their sleeves. They let their characters speak, but they don't expect us to agree with what they say – in fact, they intend us to laugh at them. This is true of some of the poems in this section and as you read you will have to decide which they are.

However, poets may also choose to write in the first-person because it enables them to reveal thoughts that would not normally be expressed and through them we are taken more deeply into a character's inner life.

Suggestions for reading the poems

Because all these poems are written in the first-person, each should be read by a single reader, with the exception of *How Many Miles*, which can be split between two readers, one asking the questions and the other giving the replies. There should be some attempt to convey the character of the speaker in each poem. For instance, the Executive should be brash and conceited, the Doctor hesitant, the Girl quiet and reflective, and the Tight-rope Walker serious and tense.

Gower Delivery

For the last hot hour or more,   **Delivery-boy**
I have been carrying boxes
To the top step, the ninth step,
Of the front door of this exclusive,
Seaside, mock Miami Beach hotel.
Once again, up into the rancid
Back of my van; checking cold boxes
of scampi, cod, mixed vegetables,
Plaice, hake, French fries and slabs of meat,
Against the journey-crumpled
Delivery-note. The frozen foods
Thawing in the furnace of the van.
Once more, I struggle back up the
Crunching gravel path. A woman
Guest, as desirable as an iced lager,
Smiles from a high, sun-demanding balcony.
Two bold children, their ice-cream cones dripping
In the mischievous heat, hurry
Down the quaking path to the crowded
Beach: the dead sky shrouds sea and sand.
Back to my sea-blue van – with the painted,
Smiling fish and short-haired, apple-cheeked
Butchers on its doors. The sun has gone mad!
I guzzle the last sour drops
Of lukewarm Coca Cola in my can,
Wipe my wet brow in my shirt-sleeves
and stoop down to re-tie a limp shoelace.
Glancing up at the balcony,
I find my golden Eve has gone.
Then the front door opens and she comes out,
Her tanned body testing her bikini's strength.
Smiling, she moves to the car park
And gets into a dark red sportscar.
I return to the burning hotel
For a man's unruly signature.

Peter Thabit Jones

Unfold Carefully

So many things get folded **Girl**
to smaller and smaller dimensions
for one or another reason:
letters for envelopes,
linen for easy storage,
newsprint for letter-boxes.
All of them utterly useless
until they are opened.

I, being folded so often,
pigeon-holed by reduction,
no longer escape the creases;
never become the letter
that illuminates friendship,
the linen cool to the sleeper,
the newspaper where my news
shout their communication.

It would be good to unfold
just once, if only to see myself
restored to my true proportions.
Besides how can I tell
what might not unfold with me,
what might not be lying in wait
for the moment of liberation
when the heart breaks open? *Cathleen Herbert*

The Watcher

I am a watcher; and the things I watch **Watcher**
Are birds and love.

Not the more common sorts of either kind.
Not sparrows, nor

Young couples. Such successful breeds are blessed
By church and state,

Surviving in huge quantities. I like
The rare Welsh kite,

Clinging to life in the far Radnor hills;
The tiny wren,

Too small for winter; and the nightingale,
Chased from her home

By bulldozers and speculating men.
In human terms,

The love I watch is rare, its habitat
Concealed and strange.

The very old, the mad, the failures. These
Have secret shares

Of loving and of being loved. I can't
Lure them with food,

Stare at them through binoculars, or join
Societies

That will preserve them. Birds are easier
To do things for.

But love is so persistent, it survives
With no one's help.

Like starlings in Trafalgar Square, cut off
By many miles

From life-supporting trees, finding their homes
On dirty roofs,

So these quiet lovers, miles from wedding bells,
Cherish their odd

And beastly dears with furtive fondling hands
And shamefaced looks,

Finding their nesting-place in hospitals
And prison cells. *U. A. Fanthorpe*

The Bicycle

There was a bicycle, a fine
Raleigh with five gears
And racing handlebars.
It stood at the front door
Begging to be mounted;
The frame shone in the sun.

I became like a character
In *The Third Policeman*, half
Human, half bike, my life
A series of dips and ridges,
Happiness a free-wheeling
Past fragrant hawthorn hedges.

Cape and sou'wester streamed
With rain when I rode to school
Side-tracking the bus-routes.
Night after night I dreamed
Of valves, pumps, sprockets,
Reflectors and repair kits.

Soon there were long rides
In the country, wet week-ends
Playing snap in the kitchens
Of mountain youth hostels,
Day-runs to Monaghan,
Rough and exotic roads.

It went with me to Dublin
Where I sold it the same winter;
But its wheels still sing
In the memory, stars that turn
About an eternal centre,
The bright spokes glittering.

Cyclist

Derek Mahon

A Commonplace Day

Mother

My floor cloth has a hole in it;
I wring out the dirty water.
The kitchen floor is clean.

My husband is eating his egg;
he does not love me.
My son is eating his egg;
it is all over his chin.
He has one tooth and he loves me.

My friend has sent a card
from Cornwall. At the Land's End
waves mount and spit and crash.
It is frightening.

My son sits in his bath
and blows ripples to the end
of the tub. He has got ten toes.
So have I. We are lucky.

My daughter comes home from school
and puts on her brownie uniform.
When she smiles, she looks like her father.
She gives me a kiss and is gone.

'Your bus fare!' I call after her.
She turns and smiles and waves
and goes running, running into the dusk.
Her tunic is a brown balloon.

My husband loved me once;
he will buy me a new floor cloth.

Beata Duncan

from *Man*

Astronaut

Alone up there you're about as alone
  as a telephone operator
With the whole world talking to you;
  They even know your pulse rate,
And when you ought to make water.
  Sure.
And being in orbit gave me no new sensations either.
  You see, we'd been through it all before,
Down here in that gadget
  Which even has a revolving globe outside the porthole.
And of course you get no sense of speed,
  less than on a subway.
You are static, suspended, watching the earth turn round
  like an old cart wheel.
And you're kept busy, very:
    recording, checking, talking back
  to a computer, programming your position,
And fuel consumption: so busy, that sleep
  is the one compelling need up there;
Sleep, where your dreams alone are heavy.
Weightlessness is a wag: Puck, as you might say,
  always up to some joke or tease
taking you unawares. Like when I coughed
  And moved into my own spit, getting an eyeful,
getting my own back ... or the crumbs
which refuse to drop.
But there was nothing new up there,
  leastways not till I opened the hatch
and took that brief walk with my rocket gun ...
  It's something I didn't tell them,
Something I kept to myself,
  it had no scientific significance
Maybe even you will laugh at me
No, it wasn't fear. I would have told them that;
  But it wasn't fear, I had nothing to fear:
The capsule only forty feet away;
  My oxygen line, straight and not fouled up;
And below me: the earth turning so gently
  trailing its shawl of clouds;
And as I watched it, I felt an emotion so strong
  the tears spurted from my eyes.
It wasn't homesickness, but earthsickness;
  A yearning, like a tide inside of me;

I would have swopped the whole universe
    for any foothold on that ball of dirt
Which I wanted then, and loved
    more than I've ever wanted or loved a woman;
I desired the earth, not any part nor any person,
    But it, where I belonged: the whole was home to me.
I guess I was the first man –
    for you can't count Him as one, I suppose? –
to feel such tenderness for the whole damn place
    and any bastard on it.
No, I don't feel it any more. Well, not so intensely.
    Maybe you have to be cut off to be in contact?
Or, maybe, it's only when the body has no weight
    that love becomes the one imponderable?
But, as I say, I didn't tell them about it.

Ronald Duncan

How Many Miles

How many miles to Babylon?   **Questioner**
    Three score and ten.
Can I get there by candle light?
    Yes and back again.
Can I get there by daylight?
    If the sun gets up on time.
Can I get there by star light?
    If they don't forget to shine.
Can I get there by electric light?
    Yes if you've been switched on.
Can I get there by torch light?
    If your batteries last that long.
What do I need to get there?
    Take everything you've got.
Everything I've gathered?
    That isn't such a lot.
So tell me how to begin.
    But that's the easiest part.
Which isn't any answer.
    You start from where you start.
And if I'm at a cross-roads?
    Try both ways at once.
They've taken down the sign-posts.
    Then try uncommon sense.
But what will I find when I get there?
    No one can tell you that.
Will it be worth the trouble?
    Tell us when you get back.
What if I stayed in Babylon?
    Nobody stays there long.
So what's the matter with Babylon?
    Just not where you belong.
And when I get back from Babylon?
    We may not know your name.
Is that what happens in Babylon?
    That nothing is ever the same.
How long could it possibly take me?
    Three score years and ten.
I don't want to waste a lifetime.
    You'll not get another again.
But I want to know what I'm in for!
    You'll not get to Babylon then.   *Gael Turnbull*

Notes on the Way to the Block

The Condemned

There's a good crowd here today
to see me off.
I never knew I had so many friends
or enemies. I see several
familiar faces, and breasts.
There's one cariad smiling
whose knickers I took off
long ago in West Tredegar.
I don't see anyone crying.

Well, now to get down
off this bloody cart.
A few in the crowd
give me a helping hand,
eager to speed my departure.
Nice of them. I never knew
I had so many friends.

The sun is shining
but the birds have gone.
Birds can sense a bad scene.
The crowd is silent, a bit awed
but looking forward to the experience.
I mount the steps, alone,
see from the corner of my eye
the executioner approach
wearing a jester's cap and bells.
Good. We don't want black
or melancholy at a time like this.

His axe looks sharp.
I give him a cigar to make it clean and quick.
Don't I get a last request
like a joint or a slug of whisky?

Someone in the crowd giggles,
but I can hear one woman weeping.
I take a last look at the sky.

John Tripp

Family Entertainment

One of the Crowd

A nice evening for it. The firemen
Look in their yellow helmets
Just like the seven dwarfs.

Blue sky, green trees, red fire.
The ladies in the crowd wear floral
Dresses and sandals, the children less.

The dogs are well-behaved, lying
On the grass and panting politely. We
Behave well, too, taking care

Not to block anyone's view. We don't
Intrude on the group by the ambulance,
We preserve a proper distance

From the hosepipes and sirens. Fresh
From kite-watching and ball-games,
With the same detached attention,

We eye ruin. The dwarfs with their axes
Hack at the stockbroker's gothic, hand
Smoking armchairs through crazed windows.

Ashy carpet flakes over sills,
Torches wink in bedrooms, the intercom
Mutters away to itself. A hose leaks.

A neighbour runs past with a basin
And towels. Some of us imagine
The losses and injuries, but no one

Cares to find out. We are simply
A crowd, whose part is to watch.
The house will be ready again

For tomorrow's performance, the wounds
Washed off. Only, as we wander away,
We sniff the scorching in our own kitchens.

U. A. Fanthorpe

Dinner Duty

Teacher

I glance from an upstairs window
To the centre of a cheering circle
Where two boys fight. I go downstairs to intervene.
Outside the door I pause to answer a question,
A girl runs up and asks,
'What's the matter, sir, are you scared?'
I walk to the screaming wall,
Break through, and finding
The loser, prone and sobbing,
Ask a boy to help me lift him up,
But get, 'I'm not helping him'.
I ask what happened.
'It was a fair fight and he lost,
Then six others came and kicked him in.'
I think of what the girl said.
Incomprehension turns to anger.
There was no concern in that girl's eyes,
No compassion in the voice of the boy.
This is the unspeakable side of teaching.
I sweep it into another poem.

Frank Wood

Funambulist

I work on a slender strand   **Tight-rope Walker**
Slung between two poles
Braced fifteen feet apart.
My patient father coached me
From childhood to fall unhurt,
Then set me again and again
On a crude slack-rope he rigged
Out back of our caravan,
Raising the rope by inches:
Now, I'm the only acrobat
In the world to include in his act,
As finale, a one-hand-stand
Thirty feet from the ground
With no net. I married
A delicate, lithe girl
From another circus family.
We are very happy. She stands
On the circular platform top
Of one pole, to steady me
As I reach the steep, last,
Incredibly difficult slope
Near the pole: when I turn about
To retrace my steps, no matter
How quickly I spin, she is there
At the top of the opposite pole,
Waiting, her arms outstretched.   *Richard Outram*

Night Sorting in Victoria

When I finish one A-to-Z pile   **Night Sorter**
another sack spills on the bench,
emptied by a silent man with a crooked smile.
Envelopes for Stoke and Bethesda,
thin packets to foreign parts
flip into pigeon-holes,
thumb and finger flicking them
like dealing cards. A long line of men
shoot good and bad news into slots.

Under powerful striplamps
the big room hums with trolleys,
a racket of whistling drivers
           loading on the ramp,
    and shouting postmen
throwing parcels marked Fragile.
The old 'surgeon' in a glass box
tries to sellotape a ruined package –
a tube of Smarties lies open on the floor.
The fast sorters with snooker-hall pallors
           work at twice our own speed,
slotting the envelopes in a buff-and-white blur.
The interest of a thousand addresses
and the race against the clock
combine to kill boredom.
At midnight we knock off for supper.

It goes on like this until dawn,
clearing the stacked bulging bags
till the last one has gone.
Then a floorwalker nods his approval
and a chargirl brings round the tea.

My wrist aches from eight hours
of sending letters on their way,
my eyes prick from squinting at scrawls.
Sorters droop along the line
like rowers after a boat race;
even the whistlers have stopped.
Half-asleep
         askew in a corner
           with the other lost bundles
I hear the first train rattle out,
see through a high grimy window
the first light creep down a winter sky.

John Tripp

A Song of the G.P.O.

Stamp-machine Man

I'm the bloke that's trained to sit behind the public stamp machines
When you come to post a letter in the rain.
   'Ow I laugh to 'ear the curses
   As they fiddle in their purses
For a 10p piece that won't pop out again.

It's me job to put the rolls of stamps behind the little slot
So you get one when you pokes your money through.
   'Ow I giggle at the slangin'
   And the nasty-tempered bangin'
If it don't come out when it's supposed to do.

If the stamp machines gets busy I put up me 'empty' signs,
Then I makes the tea and 'as me little snack,
   But the stream of filthy language
   Doesn't put me off me sangwidge
'Cos I'm taught to smile and *never* answer back.

Now, the *proper* way to buy a stamp is from the counter clerk,
Who provides a queue where you can 'ang about;
   If you don't know any better
   Than to write yer flippin' letter
After five, then you deserve to go without.

Gerry Hamill

Executive

Executive

I am a young executive. No cuffs than mine are cleaner;
I have a Slimline brief-case and I use the firm's Cortina.
In every roadside hostelry from here to Burgess Hill
The *maîtres d'hôtel* all know me well and let me sign the bill.

You ask me what it is I do. Well actually, you know,
I'm partly a liaison man and partly P.R.O.
Essentially I integrate the current export drive
And basically I'm viable from ten o'clock till five.

For vital off-the-record work – that's talking transport-wise –
I've a scarlet Aston-Martin – and does she go? She flies!
Pedestrians and dogs and cats – we mark them down for slaughter.
I also own a speed-boat which has never touched the water.

She's built of fibre-glass, of course. I call her 'Mandy Jane'
After a bird I used to know – No soda, please, just plain –
And how did I acquire her? Well to tell you about that
And to put you in the picture I must wear my other hat.

I do some mild developing. The sort of place I need
Is a quiet country market town that's rather run to seed.
A luncheon and a drink or two, a little *savoir faire* –
I fix the Planning Officer, the Town Clerk and the Mayor.

And if some preservationist attempts to interfere
A 'dangerous structure' notice from the Borough Engineer
Will settle any buildings that are standing in our way –
The modern style, sir, with respect, has really come to stay.

John Betjeman

Doctor Christmas

Doctor

My first thought: 'Have they sterilised the beard
Worn by so many Father Christmases
Before me?' Then: 'These children, they've just heard
My voice ... their doctor's voice on a ward round ...
And seen my smile; they'll notice who it is
Under the outfit, when I come again
As Father Christmas; well, here goes ...' No sound
Escapes my lips at the first bed; small fingers
Reach for the offered joy; each counterpane
Becomes a magic carpet. A fat boy
Gives me a wink: 'I've seen you!' His glance lingers
On mine. 'Today?' – but that's not what he meant;
'No; last year, at Christmas'. Grabbing his toy,
He thanks and greets me as a long-lost saint.

Edward Lowbury

Explanations

The Bicycle

The Third Policeman   a book by Flann O'Brien

Notes on the Way to the Block

cariad   darling

Some questions on the poems

1. By what details and incidents does the poet make us feel the heat of the day in *Gower Delivery*? What contrasts to the heat does he also introduce?

2. What does Cathleen Herbert mean in her poem (*Unfold Carefully*) by 'being folded so often'? By contrast, what would you imagine her to be like if she were restored to her 'true proportions'?

3. Why is the Doctor worried when the fat boy says 'I've seen you'?

4. The Mother in *A Commonplace Day* feels both satisfaction and dissatisfaction. What causes her to have these opposite feelings?

5. What, for the Teacher, is the 'unspeakable side of teaching'? What does he mean when he says 'I sweep it into another poem'?

6. The Night Sorter uses some very good descriptive language in his poem. For instance, 'a silent man with a crooked smile' and 'thumb and finger flicking them like dealing cards'. Can you quote some other examples of good descriptive detail from the poem?

7. Why do you think the wife of the Tight-rope Walker is given such importance in the poem?

8. What do you think Babylon represents in Gael Turnbull's poem (*How Many Miles*)?

Looking more closely at *Executive*

9
a) Why do you think John Betjeman was interested in creating this character?
b) By ordinary standards, the speech of the Executive is rather posh and affected – full of the jargon used in his line of business. He says 'hostelry' for 'pub' and uses phrases like 'well actually, you know'. Can you quote some more examples of his particular style of language?
c) Why do you think the speedboat had 'never touched the water'?
d) The business techniques of the Executive are revealed in the last two verses of the poem. He is a *property developer*, but he runs up against opposition from *preservationists*. Make sure that you have understood the meaning of these two expressions, then describe in more detail how the Executive goes about his profitable business.

Looking more closely at the poem about the Astronaut

10
a) We normally think of astronauts as lonely beings hurtling through space, experiencing fantastic sensations. But it wasn't like that for this astronaut. Why not? Why isn't he more excited?
b) What do we learn about the Astronaut's character from the 'brief walk' he took?
c) 'Earthsickness' is a new word. What feelings about the Earth did the Astronaut have when he was in space?
d) What does he mean by 'Maybe you have to be cut off to be in contact'?

Talking points

Which of these poems do you think were true expressions of the poet's own experience?

Which do you think were spoken by characters invented by the poets?

How can you tell the difference?

Ideas for writing

1. The poems in this section are written as though someone is thinking aloud. Try writing a 'thinking aloud' poem in which you express your own thoughts or those of an imaginary character. Here are some suggestions:

   thoughts of a character you want to make fun of;
   thoughts of a person in a dangerous situation;
   thoughts based on a strong feeling such as hate,
    jealousy, love, fear, anxiety, injustice;
   thoughts while you are doing a job;
   thoughts of a teacher or a pupil in a school situation.

2. Have you ever enjoyed owning something, as Derek Mahon enjoyed owning his bicycle? If you have, write about it in a non-rhyming poem. When did you get it? What was it like? What pleasure did you get from it? What eventually happened to it?

3. Think of some of the machines into which we put money in exchange for goods such as drinks, chocolate, soap powder and tickets. Are there people behind these machines who are determined to annoy the public, like the Stamp-machine Man? If you think there are, write a poem in which they express their points of view.

4. U. A. Fanthorpe begins her poem with 'I am a watcher ...' and describes her interest in birds and love. Begin your own poem with this same phrase and develop it in a way that shows what you find interesting to observe in animals, places and people.

5. Questions and answers form the pattern of *How Many Miles*. Attempt a poem based on a similar pattern (though not necessarily rhymed), selecting two interesting characters as the speakers.

6 We have all been in a crowd at one time or another – at a football match, on a beach, watching a procession or parade in the street, at a fairground ... to name but a few. Choose a situation in which you were one of the crowd and describe what happened and how you felt at the time.

7 Make a list of the poems from this section which you found interesting or pleasurable to read. Write an introductory paragraph on the poems in general (stating that they are all 'first-person' poems), then write a paragraph on each poem, giving your reasons for choosing it. In a final paragraph, say what you think is gained by a poem being written in the first-person style.

Bush Ballads

The early settlers in Australia in the late eighteenth century took with them the folk poetry of the countries they had left – especially England, Ireland and Scotland. They began writing songs in the folk tradition, but their subjects became the characters who were peopling the new continent – men like Jim Jones, transported to Botany Bay for poaching in England. These were the tough stories in verse, but there were more gentle ones too, and more humorous, like the love of Willie and Nancy in *The Banks of the Condamine*.

These bush songs told stories, but they were not, strictly speaking, bush ballads, which were written later, towards the end of the nineteenth century. Many of the ballad writers were of Scottish origin and were continuing the tradition of their own country by telling dramatic stories of action in simple, bold language; but the feuds of the Border country were replaced by the dramas of the outback, like the hunting down of the outlaw Ben Hall. One of the best ballad writers was 'Banjo' Paterson, the author of *Waltzing Matilda*. We see his gift at work in the humorous tales of *A Bush Christening* and *Mulga Bill's Bicycle*.

Taken together, the songs and ballads of the bush present a portrait of a growing nation – the rugged settlers who were taming the wilderness, bringing banditry within the rule of law, and developing a love of the land that was to be the foundation of the new Australia.

Suggestions for reading the poems

Jim Jones at Botany Bay	Three parts: Jim Jones, Jury, Judge.
The Ballad of Jack Lefroy	Three parts: Jack Lefroy, first speaker, second speaker, plus the Chorus (all).
The Drover's Dream	A separate reader for each verse.
The Banks of the Condamine	Two readers: Willie and Nancy.
The Death of Ben Hall	Three readers: narrator, stockman, sergeant; or ten readers: nine taking two verses each and the tenth the final verse.
If Morgan Knew	Three readers: narrator, Morgan, the boobook; or a separate reader for each of the seven verses.
The Mailman's Ride	The poem can be divided up for five readers as follows: verses 1–5, 6–8, 9–11, 12–15, 16–19.
A Bush Christening	Five readers: narrator, the boy, his father and mother, and the priest.
Mulga Bill's Bicycle	Three parts: narrator, shop assistant, Mulga Bill; or a separate reader for each of the six verses.

Jim Jones at Botany Bay

O, listen for a moment lads, and hear me tell my tale –
How, o'er the sea from England's shore I was compelled to sail.
The jury says, 'He's guilty, sir,' and says the judge, says he –
'For life, Jim Jones, I'm sending you across the stormy sea;
And take my tip before you ship to join the Iron-gang,
Don't be too gay at Botany Bay, or else you'll surely hang –
Or else you'll hang,' he says, says he – 'and after that, Jim Jones,
High up upon the gallow-tree the crows will pick your bones –
You'll have no chance for mischief then; remember what I say,
They'll flog the poaching out of you, out there at Botany Bay.'

The winds blew high upon the sea, and the pirates came along,
But the soldiers on our convict ship were full five hundred strong.
They opened fire and somehow drove that pirate ship away.
I'd have rather joined that pirate ship than come to Botany Bay:
For night and day the irons clang, and like poor galley slaves
We toil, and toil, and when we die must fill dishonoured graves.
But by and by I'll break my chains: into the bush I'll go,
And join the brave bushrangers there – Jack Donohoo and Co.;
And some dark night when everything is silent in the town
I'll kill the tyrants, one and all, and shoot the floggers down:
I'll give the Law a little shock: remember what I say,
They'll yet regret they sent Jim Jones in chains to Botany Bay.

Anon.

The Ballad of Jack Lefroy

Come all you lads and listen, a story I would tell,
Before they take me out and hang me high,
My name is Jack Lefroy, and life I would enjoy,
But the old judge has sentenced me to die.
My mother she was Irish and she taught me at her knee,
But to steady work I never did incline,
As a youngster I could ride any horse was wrapped in hide,
And when I saw a good 'un he was mine.

CHORUS So all young lads take warning and don't be led astray,
For the past you never, never can recall;
While young your gifts employ, take a lesson from Lefroy,
Let his fate be a warning to you all.

'Go straight, young man,' they told me when my first long stretch was done,
'If you're jugged again you'll have yourself to thank;'
But I swore I'd not be found hunting nuggets in the ground
When the biggest could be picked up in the bank.
Well, I've stuck up some mail-coaches, and I've ridden with Ben Hall,
And they never got me cornered once until
A pimp was in their pay gave my dingo-hole away,
And they run me down to earth at Riley's Hill.

'Come out, Lefroy!' they called me, 'come out, we're five to one!'
But I took my pistols out and stood my ground.
For an hour I pumped out lead till they got me in the head,
And when I awoke they had me bound.
It's a pleasant day to live, boys, a gloomy one to die,
A-dangling with your neck inside a string –
How I'd like to ride again down the hills to Lachlan Plain!
But when the sun rises I must swing.

Anon.

The Drover's Dream

I was travelling with the sheep, all my mates were fast asleep,
No moon or stars to illuminate the sky,
I was dozing I suppose, and my eyes did hardly close
When a very strange procession passed me by.

First there came a kangaroo with his swag of blankets blue:
He had with him a dingo for a mate.
They saluted as they passed, said they had travelled fast,
And they must be joggin' on, it's gettin' late.

Then three frogs from out the swamp, where the atmosphere was damp,
Came out and gently sat upon a stone.
They unrolled their little swags, took from out their dilly-bags
The violin, the banjo and the bone.

And a little bandicoot played a tune upon his flute,
Three native bears came down and formed a ring.
The pelican and the crane flew in from off the plain
And amused the audience with a Highland fling.

The possum and the crow sang us songs of long ago,
While the frill-necked lizard listened with a smile;
And the emu standing near with his claw up to his ear
Said, 'Funniest thing I've heard for quite a while!'

The goanna and the snake and the adder wide awake
With the alligator danced 'The Soldier's Joy'.
In the spreading silky oak the jackass cracked a joke,
And the magpie sang 'The Wild Colonial Boy'.

Some brolgas darted out from the tea-tree all about
And performed a set of Lancers very well.
Then the parrot green and blue gave the orchestra its cue
To strike up 'The Old Log Cabin in the Dell'.

I was dreaming, I suppose, of these entertaining shows,
But it never crossed my mind I was asleep,
Till the boss beneath the cart woke me up with such a start,
Yelling, 'Clancy, where the hell are all the sheep?'

W. Tully

The Banks of the Condamine

Oh, hark the dogs are barking, love,
I can no longer stay.
The men are all gone mustering
And it is nearly day,
And I must be off by the morning light
Before the sun doth shine
To meet the Sydney shearers
On the banks of the Condamine.

Oh, Willie, dearest Willie,
I'll go along with you,
I'll cut off all my auburn fringe
And be a shearer, too,
I'll cook and count your tally, love,
While ringer-o you shine,
And I'll wash your greasy moleskins
On the banks of the Condamine.

Oh, Nancy, dearest Nancy,
With me you cannot go,
The squatters have given orders, love,
No woman should do so;
Your delicate constitution
Is not equal unto mine,
To stand the constant tigering
On the banks of the Condamine.

Oh, Willie, dearest Willie,
Then stay back home with me,
We'll take up a selection
And a farmer's wife I'll be.
I'll help you husk the corn, love,
And cook your meals so fine
You'll forget the ram-stag mutton
On the banks of the Condamine.

Oh, Nancy, dearest Nancy,
Please do not hold me back,
Down there the boys are waiting,
And I must be on the track;
So here's a good-bye kiss, love,
Back home here I'll incline
When we've shore the last of the jumbucks
On the banks of the Condamine.

Anon.

The Death of Ben Hall

Ben Hall was out on the Lachlan side
With a thousand pounds on his head;
A score of troopers were scattered wide
And a hundred more were ready to ride
Wherever a rumour led.

They had followed his track from the Weddin heights
And north by the Weelong yards;
Through dazzling days and moonlit nights
They had sought him over their rifle-sights,
With their hands on their trigger-guards.

The outlaw stole like a hunted fox
Through the scrub and stunted heath,
And peered like a hawk from his eyrie rocks
Through the waving boughs of the sapling box
On the troopers riding beneath.

His clothes were rent by the clutching thorn
And his blistered feet were bare;
Ragged and torn, with his beard unshorn,
He hid in the woods like a beast forlorn,
With a padded path to his lair.

But every night when the white stars rose
He crossed by the Gunning Plain
To a stockman's hut where the Gunning flows,
And struck on the door three swift light blows,
And a hand unhooked the chain –

And the outlaw followed the lone path back
With food for another day;
And the kindly darkness covered his track
And the shadows swallowed him deep and black
Where the starlight melted away.

But his friend had read of the Big Reward,
And his soul was stirred with greed;
He fastened his door and window-board,
He saddled his horse and crossed the ford,
And spurred to the town at speed.

You may ride at a man's or a maid's behest
When honour or true love call
And steel your heart to the worst or best,
But the ride that is ta'en on a traitor's quest
Is the bitterest ride of all.

A hot wind blew from the Lachlan bank
And a curse on its shoulder came;
The pine-trees frowned at him, rank on rank,
The sun on a gathering storm-cloud sank
And flushed his cheek with shame.

He reined at the Court; and the tale began
That the rifles alone should end;
Sergeant and trooper laid their plan
To draw the net on a hunted man
At the treacherous word of a friend.

False was the hand that raised the chain
And false was the whispered word:
'The troopers have turned to the south again,
You may dare to camp on the Gunning Plain.'
And the weary outlaw heard.

He walked from the hut but a quarter-mile
Where a clump of saplings stood
In a sea of grass like a lonely isle;
And the moon came up in a little while
Like silver steeped in blood.

Ben Hall lay down on the dew-wet ground
By the side of his tiny fire;
And a night-breeze woke, and he heard no sound
As the troopers drew their cordon round –
And the traitor earned his hire.

And nothing they saw in the dim grey light,
But the little glow in the trees;
And they crouched in the tall cold grass all night,
Each one ready to shoot at sight,
With his rifle cocked on his knees.

When the shadows broke and the dawn's white sword
Swung over the mountain wall,
And a little wind blew over the ford,
A sergeant sprang to his feet and roared:
'In the name of the Queen, Ben Hall!'

Haggard, the outlaw leapt from his bed
With his lean arms held on high.
'Fire!' And the word was scarcely said
When the mountains rang to a rain of lead –
And the dawn went drifting by.

They kept their word and they paid his pay
Where a clean man's hand would shrink;
And that was the traitor's master-day
As he stood by the bar on his homeward way
And called on the crowd to drink.

He banned no creed and he barred no class,
And he called to his friends by name;
But the worst would shake his head and pass
And none would drink from the bloodstained glass
And the goblet red with shame.

And I know when I hear the last grim call
And my mortal hour is spent,
When the light is hid and the curtains fall
I would rather sleep with the dead Ben Hall
Than go where that traitor went.

Will H. Ogilvie

If Morgan Knew

When Morgan crossed the Murray to Peechelba and doom
A sombre silent shadow rode with him through the gloom.
The wild things of the forest slunk from the outlaw's track,
The boobook croaked a warning, 'Go back, go back, go back!'
It woke no answering echo in Morgan's blackened soul,
As onward through the darkness he rode towards his goal.

An evil man was Morgan, a price was on his head;
The simple bush-folk whispered his very name with dread;
Before the fierce Dan Morgan the bravest man might quake –
A cold and callous killer, he killed for killing's sake.
Past swamp and creek and gully, and settler's lone abode,
Towards the station homestead the grim Dan Morgan rode.

And still that hooded horseman that Morgan could not see,
Watched by the wild bush-creatures, rode close beside his knee.
Before them in a clearing a drover's campfire burned:
The phantom rode with Morgan, and turned when Morgan turned.
And loud the boobook's warning came on the cold night air,
'Go back, go back, Dan Morgan. Beware, beware, beware!'

He reached the station homestead; into the hall he strode,
And on his evil features the flickering lamplight glowed.
'Into one room!' he thundered. 'Bring me a glass of grog!
If any disobey me I'll shoot him like a dog!'
With pistols cocked and ready, dark-eyed and beetle-browed –
Before the famous outlaw the bravest hearts were cowed.

All night with loaded pistols he dozed and muttered there,
All night the evil shadow stood close beside his chair.
The brave Scotch girl McDonald, a lass who knew no fear,
Slipped out unseen by Morgan to warn the homesteads near.
And in the hours of darkness, before the break of dawn,
Around the fierce Dan Morgan the fatal net was drawn.

Day broke upon the Murray, the morning mists were gone,
The magpies sang their matins, the river murmured on.
When Morgan left the homestead and neared the stockyard gate
He heard the boobook's warning, and turned but turned too late –
For Quinlan pressed the trigger as Morgan swung around,
And sent the grim bushranger blaspheming to the ground.

So fell the dread Dan Morgan in Eighteen sixty-five,
In death as much unpitied as hated when alive.
He lived by blood and plunder, an outlaw to the end;
In life he showed no mercy, in death he left no friend.
And all who seek to follow in Morgan's evil track
Should heed the boobook's warning: 'Go back, go back, go back!'

Edward Harrington

The Mailman's Ride

I scanned the dark and lowering sky
That lined the sullen west,
And wondered if the storm would break
Ere I reached home and rest.
I'd ridden long and far that day
From dawn to setting sun,
My horse was failing in his strides
And he was all but done.

The air was still and sweltering hot,
The road-dust thick and red,
No wind to stir the silent trees,
And all bush life seemed dead.
Great storm-clouds gathered in the west,
Now ominous and black;
I dreaded lest the storm should sweep
And raise the creek to torrents deep
Upon my homeward track.

I had some miles to travel yet
And still some creeks to cross
And anxiously with heel and spur
I urged my weary horse;
The wind now started sighing through
The tall gums overhead –
A horseman galloped down the slope,
A led horse pulling on the rope,
And stopped on just ahead.

He pulled up in a cloud of dust,
His horses flecked with foam,
And said, 'I thought I'd meet you back
A few miles nearer home.
There is no time to lose!' he said
While springing to the ground –
He changed the saddle off the hack
And placed it on the other's back
And then turned quickly round:

'Jump on this horse and gallop on
As fast as you can ride,
Your wife's took bad, the doctor's there –
You're wanted home,' he cried.
'I'll take the mailbags and your horse,
But mount and do not wait,
Don't spare the horse but travel fast,
The horse is fresh and he will last,
Or you may be too late.'

I mounted then and wheeled around
And galloped up the rise,
A deep foreboding in my heart
And salt tears in my eyes.
I wondered what was wrong at home
And if I'd be in time,
I forced along the gallant steed,
His racing hoofs seemed slow indeed
When on the long hill climb.

We crossed the hilltops as the storm,
Long threatening, now came down,
And well I knew the creek would flood
Betwixt me and the town.
No torrents wild nor rushing streams
Would stop me winning through;
With anxious thoughts to spur me on,
A willing horse to ride upon,
No slackening rein I drew.

The sweeping storm raged through the trees,
The blinding rain beat hard
And cracking trees and rending limbs
Endangered every yard;
I heeded not the howling storm
Nor roaring creek below,
I noticed not the lightning bright
Nor yet the darkness of the night,
But faster tried to go.

We reached the grassy banks that guide
The deep creek on its course
And down the slippery bank I rode,
The swirling stream to cross;
The mountain torrent rushing down
Was turbulent and black –
No time to falter or to think,
A moment's pause upon the brink:
In plunged the gallant hack.

I tried to keep his head upstream
And face the rushing tide
As we were sweeping down and fought
To reach the other side;
I'd slipped from off the saddle's seat
To give the horse a show;
With firm hand on the bridle rein,
The other twisted in his mane,
We reached the bank below.

The timbered bank was thick and dense
And difficult to climb
I helped the horse and led him through
And lost but little time.
I mounted as I reached the road
And off again we flew.
The flashing lightning lit the way –
It was at times as bright as day –
And we were winning through.

We swept along the timbered flat
(The flat was in a flood)
And galloped up the sloping rise
And floundered through the mud;
Just one more creek to cross and then
We're on the homeward track,
But on the bank I held my breath,
To try to cross seemed courting death
But I could not hold back.

The raging water, black and wild,
Was thick with drifting wood,
The white foam-caps were whirling down
And circling where we stood;
A death-trap surely this last creek,
Its seething waters high:
The chances seemed against us here –
The game horse showed no sign of fear
As logs went sweeping by.

He faced the stream and, plunging in,
Was caught by current strong
And whirled around and overturned
As we were swept along.
He fought the current inch by inch
To reach the other bank,
And 'mid the debris rushing down
I thought at times we both would drown –
And near the end he sank.

A big bend in the winding creek
Saved both as we were done –
The horse got footing on the bank
And then the fight was won.
Exhausted for a while we lay
Upon the dank wet ground,
Both thankful for the short respite,
For death came close to us that night
When we were whirling round.

At last I reached the little home,
And all seemed dark within;
No sign to tell me how things were,
I softly tiptoed in.
The little lamp was burning low
Upon the mantel bare,
The wife and youngsters sleeping sound,
I turned the light and looked around –
No sign of sickness there.

And shivering in my soaking clothes
I gazed upon the bed,
And with a start the wife woke up.
'You're late, Jack dear,' she said.
'I thought you'd stay back at the pub
And come at break of day.
I didn't keep your supper warm.
Whatever made you face the storm?
And the mailbags – where are they?'

The mailbags! I remembered then
The big amount of cash
I carried with the mail that day –
The truth came in a flash:
Some miscreant knew about it all,
And made a plan to steal
The cash, and with the 'sick wife' ruse
He gave no time to talk or choose,
He knew just how I'd feel.

I lost the contract for the mails,
And ever since that day
I've longed to meet that man again,
But he got clean away.
They found the bags but not the cash
When they searched far and wide.
The man? No trace in any form –
And when I see a coming storm
I think of that wild ride.

Anon.

A Bush Christening

On the outer Barcoo where the churches are few,
    And men of religion are scanty,
On a road never cross'd 'cept by folk that are lost
    One Michael Magee had a shanty.

Now this Mike was the dad of a ten-year-old lad,
    Plump, healthy, and stoutly conditioned;
He was strong as the best, but poor Mike had no rest
    For the youngster had never been christened.

And his wife used to cry, 'If the darlin' should die
    Saint Peter would not recognize him.'
But by luck he survived till a preacher arrived,
    Who agreed straightaway to baptize him.

Now the artful young rogue, while they held their collogue,
    With his ear to the keyhole was listenin';
And he muttered in fright, while his features turned white,
    'What the divil and all is this christenin'?'

He was none of your dolts – he had seen them brand colts,
    And it seemed to his small understanding,
If the man in the frock made him one of the flock,
    It must mean something very like branding.

So away with a rush he set off for the bush,
    While the tears in his eyelids they glistened –
'Tis outrageous,' says he, 'to brand youngsters like me;
    I'll be dashed if I'll stop to be christened!'

Like a young native dog he ran into a log,
    And his father with language uncivil,
Never heeding the 'praste', cried aloud in his haste
    'Come out and be christened, you divil!'

But he lay there as snug as a bug in a rug,
    And his parents in vain might reprove him,
Till his reverence spoke (he was fond of a joke)
    'I've a notion,' says he, 'that'll move him.'

'Poke a stick up the log, give the spalpeen a prog;
　　Poke him aisy – don't hurt him or maim him;
Tis not long that he'll stand, I've the water at hand,
　　As he rushes out this end I'll name him.

'Here he comes, and for shame! ye've forgotten the name –
　　Is it Patsy or Michael or Dinnis?'
Here the youngster ran out, and the priest gave a shout –
　　'Take your chance, anyhow, wid 'Maginnis!''

As the howling young cub ran away to the scrub
　　Where he knew that pursuit would be risky,
The priest, as he fled, flung a flask at his head
　　That was labelled 'Maginnis's Whisky'!

Now Maginnis Magee has been made a J.P.,
　　And the one thing he hates more than sin is
To be asked by the folk, who have heard of the joke,
　　How he came to be christened Maginnis!

A. B. Paterson

Mulga Bill's Bicycle

'Twas Mulga Bill, from Eaglehawk, that caught the cycling craze;
He turned away the good old horse that served him many days;
He dressed himself in cycling clothes, resplendent to be seen;
He hurried off to town and bought a shining new machine;
And as he wheeled it through the door, with air of lordly pride,
The grinning shop assistant said, 'Excuse me, can you ride?'

'See here, young man,' said Mulga Bill, 'from Walgett to the sea,
From Conroy's Gap to Castlereagh, there's none can ride like me.
I'm good all round at everything, as everybody knows,
Although I'm not the one to talk – I hate a man that blows.

'But riding is my special gift, my chiefest, sole delight;
Just ask a wild duck can it swim, a wild cat can it fight.
There's nothing clothed in hair or hide, or built of flesh or steel,
There's nothing walks or jumps, or runs, on axle, hoof, or wheel,
But what I'll sit, while hide will hold and girths and straps are tight;
I'll ride this here two-wheeled concern right straight away at sight.'

'Twas Mulga Bill, from Eaglehawk, that sought his own abode,
That perched above the Dead Man's Creek, beside the mountain road.
He turned the cycle down the hill and mounted for the fray,
But ere he'd gone a dozen yards it bolted clean away.
It left the track, and through the trees, just like a silver streak,
It whistled down the awful slope towards the Dead Man's Creek.

It shaved a stump by half an inch, it dodged a big white-box:
The very wallaroos in fright went scrambling up the rocks,
The wombats hiding in their caves dug deeper underground,
But Mulga Bill, as white as chalk, sat tight to every bound.
It struck a stone and gave a spring that cleared a fallen tree,
It raced beside a precipice as close as close could be;
And then, as Mulga Bill let out one last despairing shriek,
It made a leap of twenty feet into the Dead Man's Creek.

'Twas Mulga Bill, from Eaglehawk, that slowly swam ashore:
He said, 'I've had some narrer shaves and lively rides before;
I've rode a wild bull round a yard to win a five-pound bet,
But this was sure the derndest ride that I've encountered yet.
I'll give that two-wheeled outlaw best; it's shaken all my nerve
To feel it whistle through the air and plunge and buck and swerve.
It's safe at rest in Dead Man's Creek – we'll leave it lying still;
A horse's back is good enough henceforth for Mulga Bill.'

A. B. Paterson

Explanations

The Ballad of Jack Lefroy

jugged	caught and imprisoned
dingo-hole	hiding place

The Banks of the Condamine

mustering	rounding-up sheep
ringer	the fastest sheep shearer in a shed
moleskins	trousers
squatters	sheep station owners
tigering	bullying
selection	a piece of land granted under Australian Land Law
ram-stag mutton	tough sheep's meat
jumbucks	sheep

The Drover's Dream

drover	herder
swag	bundle
dilly-bags	small bags, often made of grass, for carrying food
bandicoot	type of rat
goanna	type of lizard
brolgas	cranes
set of Lancers	a dance (a kind of quadrille)

Morgan

boobook	an Australian owl

The Mailman's Ride

gums	gum trees

A Bush Christening

collogue	confidential talk
'praste'	priest
spalpeen	rascal
prog	prod

Mulga Bill's Bicycle

blows	boasts
wallaroos	kangaroos

Some questions on the poems

1. Jim Jones and Jack Lefroy were both criminals, but of very different kinds and they reacted differently to the punishments they were given. Can you compare them as examples of the early Australian settlers and show how they were essentially different from each other?

2. Who are the 'baddies' in these ballads? Show how the forces of law and order triumph over the criminals and outlaws, but at the same time express your own views on the characters. Which of them did you have a certain respect or sympathy for? Which of them deserved none?

3. What was life like for the womenfolk in the Australian bush? Describe the experiences of 'the Scotch girl McDonald' (*If Morgan Knew*), 'dearest Nancy' (*The Banks of the Condamine*) and the wife of the Mailman (*The Mailman's Ride*) to show the dangers, disappointments and worries they faced. You could write as if each woman herself is speaking and telling her story.

4. The ideas and standards that were shaping the new society are touched upon in some of these poems. Can you explain the questions of:
a) loyalty and treachery in *The Death of Ben Hall*;
b) trust and deception in *The Mailman's Ride*; and
c) love and separation in *The Banks of the Condamine*?

5. Which of the poems gave you the greatest sense of what it was like to be there, in the bush country, at that particular time – experiencing the life of the people, the climate, the landscape and the animals and birds? Can you give some examples of the way the writers of these poems bring the country alive in the imagination of the reader?

6. 'Banjo' Paterson obviously saw the humorous side of life in the bush. What did he find amusing about the characters he describes in *A Bush Christening* and *Mulga Bill's Bicycle*?

Looking more closely at *The Death of Ben Hall*

7
a) Which details in verse 3 give us a picture of the bush landscape through which the troopers were pursuing Ben Hall?
b) How are we made to feel that Ben Hall was a major criminal, not just a petty one?
c) What are we told about Ben Hall to make us feel that he had been on the run a long time?
d) Imagine yourself to be the stockman. Write down the thoughts that went through your head when you were deciding whether or not to betray your friend.
e) As the stockman rode to the town to betray Ben Hall, how did nature seem to show its disapproval of him (verse 9)?
f) Why do you think the poet describes the glass (verse 18) as 'bloodstained' and the goblet as 'red with shame'?
g) In the last verse, who does the poet think is the better man – Ben Hall or the stockman?
h) What do you think? Ben Hall was a 'wanted man'. The stockman betrayed his friend. One was a criminal, the other was not – in fact, he helped to bring about justice. Was one any worse than the other?

Countrywide

Is the same English spoken in all parts of the British Isles? You could answer 'yes' or 'no' and both would be right. A speaker from Cornwall can usually understand a speaker from Cumbria because they both speak English: yet each speaker will have words, expressions and a pronunciation which are special to his or her particular part of the country. These regional differences are called 'dialects'.

But dialect is not only speech – it is writing too. To acknowledge this, 'Countrywide' is a section devoted to poetry that uses dialect and reflects the life and character of the region in which it is spoken.

We start off in London with two well-known (but not fully known) cockney songs, followed by a poem that makes clever use of cockney rhyming slang. Travelling north-east, we call in at Norfolk with a poem on the countryman's startled impressions of a visit to London. Then north-west to Lancashire where we meet Albert, his parents, and the Lion which ate him. These poems were originally written as recitations for Stanley Holloway, the music hall comedian, and they make fun of the supposed thriftiness of their Lancashire characters. The Tyneside poem, *School Leaver* is more serious and touches upon the plight of many young people in that part of the country today. Getting your tongue round some of the rich expressions in the Scottish poem may be a bit of a challenge, but it will be rewarded when you follow the antics of young Gregory on the bus!

Suggestions for reading the poems

Before you read a poem aloud, read it silently and carefully to get to know what it is about and to prepare yourself for the words and expressions that might be difficult to say.

Knees Up Mother Brown!	A separate reader for each verse. The class or a small group for the choruses.
Boiled Beef and Carrots	A separate reader for each verse. Class or group for the choruses.
A Hard Day's Night	Three readers: narrator, wife, Bill Bloggs.
The Bleed'n' Sparrer	One reader, with everyone joining in the last two lines.
Up Lunnon	A separate reader for each verse.
The Lion and Albert	Five readers: narrator, Mr. and Mrs. Ramsbottom, Animal Keeper, Manager.
The Return of Albert	Four readers: narrator, Mr. and Mrs. Ramsbottom, man from the Prudential.
School Leaver	One reader.
Omnibus Edition	A single reader, or a separate reader for each verse.

Knees Up Mother Brown!

I've just been to a 'ding-dong' down dear old Brixton way,
Old Mother Brown the Pearly Queen's a hundred years today;
Oh! what a celebration! was proper lah-di-dah!
Until they roll'd the carpet up, and shouted 'Nah then, Ma!'

>Knees up Mother Brown! Well! Knees up Mother Brown!
>Under the table you must go
>Ee-i-ee-i-ee-i-oh!
>If I catch you bending
>I'll saw your leg right off.
>So, knees up, knees up!
>Don't get the breeze up
>Knees up Mother Brown.

Joe brought his concertina, and Nobby brought the beer,
And all the little nippers swung upon the chandelier!
A black-out warden passin' yell'd, 'Ma, pull down the blind,
Just look at what you're showin'' and we shouted 'Never mind!' Ooh!

>Knees up Mother Brown! Well! Knees up Mother Brown!
>Come a-long dearie let it go!
>Ee-i-ee-i-ee-i-oh!
>It's yer blooming birthday
>Let's wake up all the town!
>So, knees up, knees up!
>Don't get the breeze up
>Knees up Mother Brown.

And fat old Uncle 'Enry 'e quite enjoyed the fun,
The buttons on his Sunday pants kept bustin' one by one!
But still 'e kept on dancin' – another one went 'pop',
He said 'I'm goin' ter keep on till me 'round-me-'ouses' drop! Ooh!

Then old Maria Perkins, she danced wiv all 'er might,
Each time she kicked 'er legs up we all shouted with delight,
'Lift up yer skirts Maria – my word, yer doin' fine!
And we can see yer washin' 'anging on the Siegfried Line.' Ooh!

We 'ad no 'pig's ear' glasses – but still we didn't mind,
We drank it out of 'vauses' and whatever we could find;
We toasted good ol' Nelson there 'anging by the door
And as we blew the froth at him he shouted with a roar – Ooh!

Bill drove up on 'is barrer – just like a proper 'swell'
And Mother Brown said 'Come inside and bring yer moke as well!'
It nibbled Grandad's whiskers, then started kicking out
And as Ma Brown went through the window we began to shout. Ooh!

And then old Granny Western – she 'ad a good 'blow out',
She 'ad two pints o' winkles wiv some cockles and some stout;
'I might 'ave indigestion', she murmured wiv a grunt,
'But lummy, up to now, it's all quiet on the 'Western Front'!' Ooh!

A crowd stood round the winder – they 'ad a lovely time,
The kids sat on the railin's, thought it was a pantomime;
Pa went round wiv 'is 'titfer' – collected one and three,
We shouted 'Come on, Mother, show 'em your agilitee.' Ooh!

Harry Weston

Boiled Beef and Carrots

When I was a nipper only six months old,
My mother and my father too,
They didn't know what to wean me on,
They were both in a dreadful stew;
They thought of tripe, they thought of steak,
Or a little bit of old cod's roe,
I said, 'Pop round to the old cookshop,
I know what'll make me grow'.

> Boiled beef and carrots,
> Boiled beef and carrots,
> That's the stuff for your 'Darby-kel',
> Makes you fat and it keeps you well,
> Don't live like vegetarians,
> On food they give to parrots,
> From morn till night blow out your kite on
> Boiled beef and carrots.

When I got married to Eliza Brown,
A funny little girl next door,
We went to Brighton for the week,
Then we both toddled home once more;
My pals all met me in the pub,
Said a fellow to me, 'What cher, Fred,
What did you have for your honeymoon?'
So just for a lark I said: (CHORUS)

We've got a lodger, he's an artful cove,
'I'm very very queer,' he said.
We sent for the doctor, he came round,
And he told him to jump in bed.
The poor chap said, 'I do feel bad',
Then my mother with a tear replied,
'What would you like for a 'Pick me up'?'
He jumped out of bed and cried: (CHORUS)

I am the father of a lovely pair
Of kiddies, and they're nice fat boys;
They're twins, you can't tell which is which,
Like a pair of saveloys.
We had them christened in the week.
When the Parson put them on his knee,
I said, 'as they've got ginger hair,
Now I want their names to be: (CHORUS)

Charles Collins

A Hard Day's Night

Bill Bloggs came home
One night and saw
His carving-knife
Was at the door.

She gave him a butcher's
From her mince pies,
And said, 'Bill Bloggs,
Don't tell me lies,
Or try to be funny,
Where's the bees and honey?
You're elephant's trunk,
I'm telling you.'

'Too Irish stew,'
Poor Bloggsey said,
'Oh, me loaf of bread.
Now just you cut
The rabbit and pork,'
And he tried to walk
Up the apples and pears.

But his bacon and eggs
Fell out with his plates,
Like they'd never been mates,
And his quaker oat
Had a fight with his throat,
And his this and that
Got flung on the mat,
And his Dicky dirt
Got grievously hurt ...

'Here, me old pot and pan,'
Said his wife, and ran,
And shoving him plumb
In the fife and drum,
She stripped him stark
In the Noah's ark,
And said, 'Bill Bloggs,
Now just you mark,
It's like I said,
I keeps yer round the houses,
And *you* keeps yer Uncle Ned.'

Anon.

The Bleed'n' Sparrer

We 'ad a bleed'n' sparrer wot
Lived up a bleed'n' spaht,
One day the bleed'n' rain came dahn
An' washed the bleeder aht.

An' as 'e layed 'arf drahnded
Dahn in the bleed'n' street
'E begged that bleed'n' rainstorm
To bave 'is bleed'n' feet.

But then the bleed'n' sun came aht –
Dried up the bleed'n' rain –
So that bleed'n' little sparrer
'E climbed up 'is spaht again.

But, Oh! – the crewel sparrer'awk,
'E spies 'im in 'is snuggery,
'E sharpens up 'is bleed'n' claws
An' rips 'im aht by thuggery!

Jist then a bleed'n' sportin' type
Wot 'ad a bleed'n' gun
'E spots that bleed'n' sparrer'awk
An' blasts 'is bleed'n' fun.

The moral of this story
Is plain to everyone –
That them wot's up the bleed'n' spaht
Don't get no bleed'n' fun.

Anon.

Up Lunnon

Laast week I went up Lunnon, bor;
O'course, I'a bin up thar afore;
That wholla fare t'maake a chaange, that dew.
But tha's no plaace fer me t'stay;
An I'm right glad t'maake m'way
Back hoom agin t'Norfolk – ah, tha's trew!

Why, tha's all go up Lunnon, bor.
There in't no time t'stand an jaw,
An dew yew try, yew can't hear what yew say.
An all that traffic go so faast,
Wi' evrabodda rushin' paast,
Dew yew stan' still, yew jus' git swept away.

An what about them blocks o' flats?
They mus' be rough on dogs an' cats;
My Towser wun't think much t'that, I know.
An livin up there in the sky –
Why, no house orter be that high;
That mus' be suffin' breezy when that blow!

When yew git in a Lunnon street
I tell yew, bor, yew feel the heat,
Yit can't see th'ole sun rise, na yit go down.
There's sky above yar hid, I doubt,
But yew can't see it all spreed out
Around yer, like that is outside the town.

An evrawhere yew go yew see
Shop winders – ah, they fare t'be
Jus' tricolaated up t'draw yar dough.
I'd suner see the baads an bees,
The open fields, an flars, an trees.
I reckon as they maake a batter show.

An all that row – ah, tha's the wust;
My poor ole hid were fit t'bust.
That fare like evrathing kick up a dullor.
An lights an signs – I'a never seen
So many – don't know what they mean;
They 'a got 'em there o' a'most evra colour!

Course, yew can travel underground;
Them tunnels maake a funna sound;
There's doors what shut an open for yer tew,
An movin' stairs – they'd be a treat,
But somehow they don't suit my feet.
Ar mudda loke feel saafer, that that dew.

An cor – them crowds, all in a hurry,
Wi' faaces what look full o' worry
As they go crowdin' paast yer on their way.
Tha's how it is, bor, all the while –
They jus' int got no time t'smile;
An so, gi'me the country enna day!

John Kett

The Lion and Albert

There's a famous seaside place called Blackpool,
    That's noted for fresh air and fun,
And Mr. and Mrs. Ramsbottom
    Went there with young Albert, their son.

A grand little lad was young Albert,
    All dressed in his best; quite a swell
With a stick with an 'orse's 'ead 'andle,
    The finest that Woolworth's could sell.

They didn't think much to the Ocean:
    The waves, they was fiddlin' and small,
There was no wrecks and nobody drownded,
    Fact, nothing to laugh at at all.

So, seeking for further amusement,
    They paid and went into the Zoo,
Where they'd Lions and Tigers and Camels,
    And old ale and sandwiches too.

There were one great big Lion called Wallace;
    His nose were all covered with scars –
He lay in a somnolent posture,
    With the side of his face on the bars.

Now Albert had heard about Lions,
  How they was ferocious and wild –
To see Wallace lying so peaceful,
  Well, it didn't seem right to the child.

So straightway the brave little feller,
  Not showing a morsel of fear,
Took his stick with its 'orse's 'ead 'andle
  And pushed it in Wallace's ear.

You could see that the Lion didn't like it,
  For giving a kind of a roll,
He pulled Albert inside the cage with 'im,
  And swallowed the little lad 'ole.

Then Pa, who had seen the occurrence,
  And didn't know what to do next,
Said 'Mother! Yon Lion's 'et Albert',
  And Mother said 'Well, I am vexed!'

Then Mr. and Mrs. Ramsbottom –
  Quite rightly, when all's said and done –
Complained to the Animal Keeper,
  That the Lion had eaten their son.

The keeper was quite nice about it;
  He said 'What a nasty mishap.
Are you sure that it's *your* boy he's eaten?'
  Pa said 'Am I sure? There's his cap!'

The manager had to be sent for.
  He came and he said 'What's to do?'
Pa said 'Yon Lion's 'et Albert,
  And 'im in his Sunday clothes, too.'

Then Mother said, 'Right's right, young feller;
  I think it's a shame and a sin,
For a lion to go and eat Albert,
  And after we've paid to come in.'

The manager wanted no trouble,
  He took out his purse right away,
Saying 'How much to settle the matter?'
  And Pa said 'What do you usually pay?'

But Mother had turned a bit awkward
  When she thought where her Albert had gone.
She said 'No! someone's got to be summonsed' –
  So that was decided upon.

Then off they went to the P'lice Station,
  In front of the Magistrate chap;
They told 'im what happened to Albert,
  And proved it by showing his cap.

The Magistrate gave his opinion
  That no one was really to blame
And he said that he hoped the Ramsbottoms
  Would have further sons to their name.

At that Mother got proper blazing,
  'And thank you, sir, kindly,' said she.
'What waste all our lives raising children
  To feed ruddy Lions? Not me!'

Marriott Edgar

The Return of Albert

You've 'eard 'ow young Albert Ramsbottom,
   In the Zoo up at Blackpool one year,
With a stick and 'orse's 'ead 'andle,
   Gave a lion a poke in the ear.

The name of the lion was Wallace,
   The poke in the ear made 'im wild;
And before you could say 'Bob's your Uncle,'
   'E'd up and 'e'd swallered the child.

'E were sorry the moment 'e'd done it,
   With children 'e'd always been chums,
And besides, 'e'd no teeth in 'is noddle,
   And 'e couldn't chew Albert on t' gums.

'E could feel the lad moving inside 'im,
   As 'e lay on 'is bed of dried ferns,
And it might 'ave been little lad's birthday,
   'E wished 'im such 'appy returns.

But Albert kept kicking and fighting,
   Till Wallace arose feeling bad,
And felt it were time that 'e started to stage
   A come-back for the lad.

So with 'is 'ead down in a corner,
   On 'is front paws 'e started to walk,
And 'e coughed and 'e sneezed and 'e gargled,
   Till Albert shot out like a cork.

Old Wallace felt better direc'ly,
   And 'is figure once more became lean,
But the only difference with Albert
   Was 'is face and 'is 'ands were quite clean.

Meanwhile Mister and Missus Ramsbottom
   'Ad gone 'ome to tea feeling blue;
Ma says 'I feel down in the mouth like,'
   Pa says 'Aye! I bet Albert does too.'

Said Ma 'It just goes for to show yer
   That the future is never revealed,
If I thought we was going to lose 'im
   I'd 'ave not 'ad 'is boots soled and 'eeled.'

'Let's look on the bright side,' said Father
   'What can't be 'elped must be endured,
Every cloud 'as a silvery lining,
   And we did 'ave young Albert insured.'

A knock at the door came that moment,
   As Father these kind words did speak,
'Twas the man from t' Prudential,
   'E'd called for their 'tuppence per person per week.'

When Father saw who 'ad been knocking,
   'E laughed and 'e kept laughing so,
That the young man said 'What's there to laugh at?'
   Pa said 'You'll laugh an' all when you know.'

'Excuse 'im for laughing,' said Mother,
   'But really things 'appen so strange,
Our Albert's been ate by a lion,
   You've got to pay us for a change.'

Said the young feller from the Prudential,
   'Now, come come, let's understand this,
You don't mean to say that you've lost 'im?'
   Ma says 'Oh, no! we *know* where 'e is.'

When the young man 'ad 'eard all the details,
   A bag from 'is pocket he drew,
And 'e paid them with int'rest and bonus,
   The sum of nine pounds four and two.

Pa 'ad scarce got 'is 'and on the money,
   When a face at the window they see,
And Mother says 'Eeh! look, it's Albert,'
   And Father says 'Aye, it *would* be.'

Young Albert came in all excited,
   And started 'is story to give,
And Pa says 'I'll never trust lions again,
   Not as long as I live.'

The young feller from the Prudential
   To pick up the money began,
And Father says 'Eeh! just a moment,
   Don't be in a hurry, young man.'

Then giving young Albert a shilling,
   He said 'Pop off back to the Zoo.
'Ere's yer stick with the 'orse's 'ead 'andle,
   Go and see what the Tigers can do!'

Marriott Edgar

School Leaver

At scheul such idealistic plans war made!
'We'll build a new Jerusalem!' they said.
O-levels? Aye! But noo Aa'm jist a lout.
Hoo can Aa larn the art of dein' nowt
When Aa wuz trained at scheul t' 'arn me bait,
And educated so Aa could create?
Y've laid on me a hopeless, blightin' curse
And med a sow's ear of a silkin purse.
Aa'll not conform nor shave nor cut me hair.
Aa 'waste me sweetness on the desert air.'
A 'mute inglorious Milton', me. Aa grieve,
Ne chance t' earn, t' build, create, achieve.
Me poverty and loss hits mair than me.
Hoo big a loss t' the community?
Nebody knaas. T' wreck the human sowl,
Train blokes t' sarve, then put them on the dole.

Fred Reed

Omnibus Edition

Come on, sonny, an' tak ma han'
We'll fairly hae tae rush
Noo, Gregory, you behave yersel'
Aince we're on the bus!

I've pit in sic a day wi' ye –
Ye've messed up a' yer claes
Noo, stan' there till I get ma purse
Alis! Get aff ma taes!

Here's the bus, so on ye jump
An' try an' get a seatie
Look, up the steps ye go, ma lad –
No, ye canna hae a sweetie!

That's richt, jist ye move alang
An' you'll get next the windie
If he disna get his special seat
He'll kick up sic a shindy.

One an' a half tae Stoorie Brae –
Oh, I'm awfu sorry, driver
Bit wi' ae thing an' anither
I've naething less than a fiver!

Och, its fine tae be sittin' doon at last
I'm feelin' fair ferfochen
Gregory, stop sookin' the toggles on yer coat
Nae muckle winder ye're chokin'.

Oh, hullo, Mrs. Smith – hoo *are* ye?
Whit a bonnie hat ye're wearin'
Gregory, turn roon' an' face the front
Its ill-mennert tae go on starin'.

Sit still an' look oot the windie
See, there's a bonnie collie dug.
I hear the Wilson's hiv hid their third –
Gregory, tak yer fingers oot yer lug!

It wis rainin' fin we left the day
The bus took lang tae come
I'm at ma man tae buy a car –
Gregory, stop crackin' that gum!

I canna stick that clairty stuff
It couldna be good tae eat
Spit it oot at aince, I tell ye –
Gregory, nae on the back o' the seat!

It fair taks it oot o' ye shoppin'
There's an awfu steer in the toon
Did ye hear aboot Jeannie's weddin'?
Gregory look – SIT DOON!

The merriage wis a bittie hurried-like –
I've heard some rumours, hiv *you*?
Gregory, if ye *maun* sing, mak it something else –
Nae 'The Big Broon Coo!'

An' the money I've gaun through the day
I'll really hae tae ca' canny
Gregory, ye impident little deil –
Stop makin' faces at that mannie!

I got a cardigan for ma mither
An' a scarf tae Beth in Montrose
They hidna muckle tae choose frae –
Gregory – stop pickin' yer nose!

Bit a'things sic an awfu price
An' the cost o' butcher meat
I bocht some chops an' a pun' o' mince –
Gregory, tak yer feet aff the seat!

This inflation's gaein' ower wir heids
Ye dinna ken wha tae blame
Gregory, whit d'ye wint tae whisper aboot?
No, ye'll hae tae wait till we get hame!

Whit's that, Mrs. Smith? They're sellin' their hoose?
Ay, a gie queer pair, it's true
Gregory, whaur's that chocolate?
Bide at peace till I dicht yer moo'.

That's richt, pet, draw floories on the gless
An' keep in your ain place
Eeeh? Whit's *that* ye've written on the pane?
Oh, whaur can I pit ma face?

Jist wait till yer father hears aboot this
He'll surely gie ye hell
The amount that's spent on schoolin' tae –
Gregory, ye canna spell!

If I'd ony mair like this, ye ken
I'd need some extra help
Gregory, if ye dinna sit doon on yer dock –
I'll gie ye a damned gweed skelp!

The time I've hid wi this ill-trickit loon
Tae describe it wirds jist fail me
An' whit he did in his wellingtons –
I hardly dare tae tell ye!

Ah, here we are – oor stop at last,
I've enjoyed wir wee bit crack
Weel, cheerio the noo, Mrs. Smith –
Gregory, stop hingin' back!

Come awa, it's time tae get aff
Go on noo, dinna scutter
Watch whaur ye're gaein', ye clumsy vratch
Ye've landit in a gutter!

Up wi' yer handie – that's the stuff –
An' wave tae the fowk on the bus
I think the driver's han's up tae –
OH! THE NERVE TAE DAE THAT TAE US!

Christina Forbes Middleton

Explanations

Knees Up Mother Brown!

ding-dong	sing song
round-me-'ouses	trousers
the Siegfried line	a German line of defence
pig's ear	beer
moke	mule
Western Front	battlefront in Western Europe
titfer (tit-fer-tat)	hat
one and three	old money, one shilling and three pennies (worth about 6p)

Boiled Beef and Carrots

Darby-kel(ly)	belly
kite	stomach
artful cove	cunning fellow

A Hard Day's Night

carving knife	wife
butcher's (hook)	look
bees and honey	money
elephant's trunk	drunk
Irish stew	true
rabbit and pork	talk
bacon and eggs	legs
plates (of meat)	feet
quaker oat	coat
this and that	hat
Dicky dirt	shirt
pot and pan	man
fife and drum	bum
Noah's Ark	dark
Uncle Ned	bed

Up Lunnon

bor	neighbour
wholla	wholly, entirely
fare	seem
dew	do
jaw	talk
yew	you
hid	head

tricolaated	decorated
dough	money
baads	birds
flars	flowers
dullor	noise
mudda loke	muddy lane
enna	any

School Leaver

noo	now
Aa'm	I'm
hoo	how
dein'	doing
'arn me bait	earn my living
mair	more
nebody knaas	nobody knows
sarve	serve

Omnibus Edition

hae tae	have to
aince	once
pit in sic	put in such
claes	clothes
taes	toes
sic a shindy	such a fuss
ferfochen	tired out
sookin'	sucking
nae muckle winder	it's no wonder
ill-mennert	ill-mannered
hiv hid	have had
lug	ear
fin	when
clairty	sticky
steer	stir, commotion
maun	must
gaun	gone
ca' canny	go carefully
deil	devil
hidna muckle	didn't have much
bocht	bought
pun'	pound
gaein' ower wir heids	going over our heads
dinna ken	don't know
gie	right

whaur	where
dicht yer moo	wipe your mouth
floories	flowers
ony mair	any more
gweed skelp	good spank
dock	bottom
loon	fool
crack	gossip
dinna scutter	don't scurry
vratch	wretch

Questions on Countrywide

1. In *Knees Up Mother Brown!* we get the feeling of a high-spirited family party and we are introduced to some amusing characters. Who exactly turned up? What details are we given about them?

2. We see in the cockney poems that rhyming slang is still a living, humorous part of the dialect. Not all the examples are explained in the glossary. Can you work out the meaning of those that are not?

3. Having translated all the rhyming slang in *A Hard Day's Night*, can you sum up what happens in the poem?

4. What do you see as being typical of these cockney songs and poems – broad humour? The enjoyment of playing with words and meanings? Odd characters? In a short piece of writing, try to explain to someone who has not read the poems what gives them their liveliness and quality.

5. Do you find yourself agreeing with the feelings expressed in *Up Lunnon* or not? Is there anything which you think the countryman has not appreciated about London – or any big city, for that matter? Write a poem yourself on what you think are the pleasures or the disadvantages of living in either a town or the country.

6 It doesn't sound like a very amusing situation – a lion in a zoo swallowing an innocent young boy; yet the Albert poems are obviously not intended to make us weep. Can you say where the humour lies in the poems and give some examples of it?

7 'Ere's yer stick with the 'orse's 'ead 'andle,
Go and see what the Tigers can do!'
– says Mr. Ramsbottom. Write about what happened when Albert returned to the zoo, either in the form of a poem or a story.

8 Writing in your own form of regional English might help you to express your thoughts more freely and directly. Try a short poem in the style of *School Leaver*, writing about yourself, as you are now.

9 Where does the comedy arise in *Omnibus Edition*? How has the style of writing helped to make the character of the mother more convincing? What aspects of the poem do you recognize as being true-to-life?

10 You have probably been introduced to a number of new dialect words and expressions through reading these poems. Make a selection from each region of those that have interested you. Can you think of any similar expressions in other dialects?

Everything Lives

'Everything lives' is a phrase taken from a Cameroon poem by an unknown writer which celebrates the life and movements of the fish, the bird and the monkey. Its companion poem, also from the Cameroon, is *Elephant Song*, a hymn to the might of the elephant and the skill of the men who hunt it.

These are just two aspects of man's relationship with the animal world which are expressed in the following poems. Others include the appreciation of character in the individual animal or bird and, at the other end of the scale, the industrialized farming systems in which all feeling for animals as individuals is lost.

Closely linked in these poems are the twin themes: the qualities animals possess as living creatures; and the various ways in which man brings about their death.

Suggestions for reading the poems

Movements	A single reader; or a separate reader for each *sentence* in the first two verses and one reader for the last verse.
Hunting a Hare	Divide the poem into sections for separate readers; verses: 1–3, 4–5, 6–7, 8–13, 14–16, 17.
Song of the Animal World	Three soloists (fish, bird, monkey); Chorus to say 'Hip! Viss! Gnan!' and the refrain: 'Everything lives, everything dances, everything chirps'.
Elephant Song	A separate reader for each verse with everyone joining in the chorus.
Pig Farm Supreme	Four readers: verses 1–2, 3–5, 6 and 7.
Milking Time	Five readers: one for each verse.
Praise of a Collie	Narrator and Pollóchan; or a separate reader for each verse.
The Early Purges	Narrator/poet and Dan.
Hen Dying	One reader.
Ella Mason and Her Eleven Cats	Two readers: narrator, people/children.
The Coral Polyp	
The Spider	One reader for each.
Turkeys	
The Butterfly	

Movements

Lark drives invisible pitons in the air
And hauls itself up the face of space.
Mouse stops being comma and clockworks on the floor.
Cats spill from walls. Swans undulate through clouds.
Eel drills through darkness its malignant face.

Fox, smouldering through the heather bushes, bursts
A bomb of grouse. A speck of air grows thick
And is a hornet. When a gannet dives
It's a white anchor falling: and when it lands
Umbrella heron becomes walking-stick.

I think these movements and become them, here,
In this room's stillness, none of them about,
And relish them all – until I think of where,
Thrashed by a crook, the cursive adder writes
Quick V's and Q's in the dust and rubs them out.

Norman MacCaig

Hunting a Hare

(To my friend Yuri)

Hunting a hare. Our dogs are raising a racket;
Racing, barking, eager to kill, they go,
And each of us in a yellow jacket
Like oranges against the snow.

One for the road. Then, off to hound a hare,
My cab driver friend who hates a cop, I,
Buggins' brother and his boy, away we tear.
Our jalopy,

That technological marvel, goes bounding,
Scuttling along on its snow chains. Tallyho!
After a hare we go.
Or is it ourselves we're hounding?

I'm all dressed up for the chase
In boots and jacket: the snow is ablaze.
But why, Yuri, why,
Do my gun sights dance? Something is wrong, I know,
When a glassful of living blood has to fly
In terror across the snow.

The urge to kill, like the urge to beget,
Is blind and sinister. Its craving is set
Today on the flesh of a hare: tomorrow it can
Howl the same way for the flesh of a man.

Out in the open the hare
Lay quivering there
Like the grey heart of an immense
Forest or the heart of silence:

Lay there, still breathing,
Its blue flanks heaving,
Its tormented eye a woe,
Blinking there on the cheek of the snow.

Then, suddenly, it got up,
Stood upright: suddenly,
Over the forest, over the dark river,
The air was shivered
By a human cry,

Pure, ultrasonic, wild,
Like the cry of a child.
I knew that hares moan, but not like this:
This was the note of life, the wail
Of a woman in travail,

The cry of leafless copses
And bushes hitherto dumb,
The unearthly cry of a life
Which death was about to succumb.

Nature is all wonder, all silence:
Forest and lake and field and hill
Are permitted to listen and feel,
But denied utterance.

Alpha and Omega, the first and the last
Word of Life as it ebbs away fast,
As, escaping the snare, it flies
Up to the skies.

For a second only, but while
It lasted we were turned to stone
Like actors in a movie-still.

The boot of the running cab driver hung in mid-air,
And four black pellets halted, it seemed,
Just short of their target:
Above the horizontal muscles,
The blood-clotted fur of the neck,
A face flashed out.

With slanting eyes set wide apart, a face
As in frescoes of Dionysus,
Staring at us in astonishment and anger,
It hovered there, made one with its cry,
Suspended in space,
The contorted transfigured face
Of an angel or a singer.

Like a long-legged archangel a golden mist
Swam through the forest.
'Shit!' spat the cab driver. 'The little faking freak!'
A tear rolled down on the boy's cheek.

Late at night we returned,
The wind scouring our faces: they burned
Like traffic lights as, without remark,
We hurtled through the dark.

Andrei Voznesensky

Song of the Animal World

SOLOIST:
    The fish goes . . . . CHORUS: Hip!
    The bird goes . . . . Viss!
    The monkey goes . . . . Gnan!

SOLOIST (*mimicking*):
    I jump to the left,
    I turn to the right,
    I'm being the fish
    That slips through the water, that slips,
    That twists, that springs!
Everything lives, everything dances, everything chirps . . .

    The fish . . . . Hip!
    The bird . . . . Viss!
    The monkey . . . . Gnan!

SOLOIST (*mimicking*):
    The bird flies away,
    Flies, flies, flies,
    Goes, comes back, passes,
    Rises, floats, swoops,
    I'm being the bird.
Everything lives, everything dances, everything chirps . . .

    The fish . . . . Hip!
    The bird. . . . . Viss!
    The monkey . . . . Gnan!

SOLOIST (*mimicking*):
    The monkey – from branch to branch
    He runs, hops, jumps,
    With his wife and his brat,
    His mouth stuffed full, his tail in the air.
    Here's the monkey, here's the monkey!
Everything lives, everything dances, everything chirps . . .

    The fish . . . . Hip!
    The bird . . . . Viss!
    The monkey . . . . Gnan!

Anon.
from the Cameroon

Elephant Song

On the weeping forest, under the evening wind,
Black night has lain down joyfully,
In the sky the stars have fled, trembling,
Fireflies that shine vaguely and go out.
Up there, the moon is dark, its white light has gone out.
The spirits are wandering.
Elephant hunter, take your bow!

CHORUS:
Elephant hunter, take your bow!

In the frightened forest the tree sleeps, leaves are dead,
Monkeys have shut their eyes, hanging high in the branches,
Antelopes slip along with silent steps,
Crop the fresh grass, prick up their ears, intent,
Raise their heads and listen, startled.
The cicada falls silent, shutting in its rasping song.
Elephant hunter, take your bow!

CHORUS:
Elephant hunter, take your bow!

In the forest lashed by a great rain,
Father Elephant walks, heavily, *bau, bau,*
At ease and fearless, sure of his strength,
Father Elephant whom none can overcome,
Breaking through the forest, he stops, starts off again.
He eats, trumpets, knocks down trees, and seeks his mate.
Father Elephant, you are heard from far away.
Elephant hunter, take your bow!

CHORUS:
Elephant hunter, take your bow!

In the forest through which no man except you goes,
Hunter, lift up your heart, slip, run, jump, walk!
Meat is before you, the huge mass of meat,
The meat that walks like a hill,
The meat that makes the heart glad,
The meat that will roast at your fire,
The meat into which your teeth sink,
The fine red meat and the blood that is drunk smoking.
Elephant hunter, take your bow!

CHORUS:
Yo-ye, elephant hunter, take your bow!
Yo-ye, elephant hunter, take your bow!

Anon.
from the Cameroon

Pig Farm Supreme

Sunday p.m. and we're up at the 'big house'
with its shorn lawns and Union Jack streaming
from a white flagpole. The porch is porticoed.
The place seems to grow out of the countryside.

Behind the house the farm spreads across Ireland.
No rusting tractor, lame hen, or pile of tyres.
No stinking dunghill steaming in the sunshine.
In Magee tweeds the manager shakes my hand.

He leads us through cathedral barns, down steep steps,
underground to the long gallery of pigs.
Here we troop past tier upon tier of cages,
each with its squash of porkers waiting the chop.

The lights are never out; nights tacked on to days.
The food, balanced to the gram, jets through tube chutes
and all the snouts go down, snuffling and snaffling.
The noise, the heat, the stink of meat beats your head.

It's *then* you see the cage floors. No straw in sight,
just iron slats through which crud pours to shower
the cells beneath. Twice daily the beasts are hosed.
The scrubbed-up pigs glow pink as candyfloss.

Back at the house we're served tea and wheaten bread
by girls with skin like ice and eyes brown as bark.
Sun burnishes the wall-length windows. The floor's
polished just enough to let you break your back.

And far, far below the pigs swell in their cells,
their lives worked out in weights and water, blood near
boiling, their endless days filled tight with screaming.
Knives are ground on stones. And it's going on now.

Wes Magee

Milking Time

Pressed warm against the cows' soft flanks
Sometimes we tilted heads to eye
The great gargantuan webs looping
The rafters; grey, ragged sheets
Draping the deeper dustier dark
Of frightened hermit spiders.

      Crick
In the neck, we'd turn to the cats;
Tease them by aiming cheeky jets
At the waiting, anxious, time-marking
Line, till baleful, bedraggled they
Broke up parade, licked insult
Away, then sulked back, one by one,
To malign us.

           Stripping the teats
We'd edge our palms, scuff from the froth
Odd hard-dung flecks and fallen bits,
Fling to the wall the muck-caked stool,
Slosh amends to the cats, and swing
Fast down 'the pass' to strain our pails
Into the large milk bowls.

           Byre smells
Seeped into hair and skin, came with
Us to school to the smart town kids
Whose education lacked our lore –
Strong healthy words like 'sharn' and 'strang'.

Now exiled in prim, pasteurised
Ways, we view strange farms from stranger
Camp site splatterings. We frown as
We double rinse our cups at stray
Specks of grass on the plastic ware.
At the barbed wire fence we stretch
Across to stroke the cows; feel once
Again soft sides, warm simple folds
That once, too safely, held our heads.

Madeline Munro

Praise of a Collie

She was a small dog, neat and fluid –
Even her conversation was tiny:
She greeted you with *bow*, never *bow-wow*.

Her sons stood monumentally over her
But did what she told them. Each grew grizzled
Till it seemed he was his own mother's grandfather.

Once, gathering sheep on a showery day,
I remarked how dry she was. Pollóchan said, 'Ah,
It would take a very accurate drop to hit Lassie.'

And her tact – and tactics! When the sheep bolted
In an unforeseen direction, over the skyline
Came – who but Lassie, and not even panting.

She sailed in the dinghy like a proper sea-dog.
Where's a burn? – she's first on the other side.
She flowed through fences like a piece of black wind.

But suddenly she was old and sick and crippled ...
I grieved for Pollóchan when he took her a stroll
And put his gun to the back of her head.

Norman MacCaig

The Early Purges

I was six when I first saw kittens drown.
Dan Taggart pitched them, 'the scraggy wee shits',
Into a bucket; a frail metal sound,

Soft paws scraping like mad. But their tiny din
Was soon soused. They were slung on the snout
Of the pump and the water pumped in.

'Sure isn't it better for them now?' Dan said.
Like wet gloves they bobbed and shone till he sluiced
Them out on the dunghill, glossy and dead.

Suddenly frightened, for days I sadly hung
Round the yard, watching the three sogged remains
Turn mealy and crisp as old summer dung

Until I forgot them. But the fear came back
When Dan trapped big rats, snared rabbits, shot crows
Or, with a sickening tug, pulled old hens' necks.

Still, living displaces false sentiments
And now, when shrill pups are prodded to drown
I just shrug, 'Bloody pups'. It makes sense:

'Prevention of cruelty' talk cuts ice in town
Where they consider death unnatural,
But on well-run farms pests have to be kept down.

Seamus Heaney

Hen Dying

The old grey hen is dying
who once was so cheeky.
For ten years or more
I've not been able to leave the house
without her begging bowl
being thrust in front of me.
You have to be in the mood for hens.
Some days I had my heart set on people.

She's learning now about queues and things
and how the spring sunshine
rests more heavily on some hens
than on others.
She sits by herself over near the byre.
Her head's pulled in like a tortoise's.
Her eyelids are half drawn-down.

The other hens have cast her out.
They batter her with their beaks
whenever they come across her.
Most of them are her daughters.
Hens are inhuman.

She doesn't visit the feed any more.
I lay some grain in front of her
whenever I come across her.
She rummages through her mind,
slowly remembering how to eat.

One of these days she'll fall over.
I'll make a coffin from a shoebox for her
and tie it with a piece of ribbon.
I'll bury her in a corner of the stackyard
between two stooks of corn.

That's holy ground to hens and crofters.
The earth is dry and sandy there
and the worm count is as low
as any place in Ardnamurchan.
For a week or two I'll miss her.

Alasdair Maclean

Ella Mason and Her Eleven Cats

Old Ella Mason keeps cats, eleven at last count,
In her ramshackle house off Somerset Terrace;
People make queries
On seeing our neighbour's cat-haunt,
Saying: 'Something's addled in a woman who accommodates
That many cats.'

Rum and red-faced as a water-melon, her voice
Long gone to wheeze and seed, Ella Mason
For no good reason
Plays hostess to Tabby, Tom and increase,
With cream and chicken-gut feasting the palates
Of finical cats.

Village stories go that in olden days
Ella flounced about, minx-thin and haughty,
A fashionable beauty,
Slaying the dandies with her emerald eyes;
Now, run to fat, she's a spinster whose door shuts
On all but cats.

Once we children sneaked over to spy Miss Mason
Napping in her kitchen paved with saucers.
On antimacassars
Table-top, cupboard shelf, cats lounged brazen,
One gruff-timbred purr rolling from furred throats:
Such stentorian cats!

With poke and giggle, ready to skedaddle,
We peered agog through the cobwebbed door
Straight into yellow glare
Of guardian cats crouched round their idol,
While Ella drowsed whiskered with sleek face, sly wits:
Sphinx-queen of cats.

'Look! there she goes, Cat-Lady Mason!'
We snickered as she shambled down Somerset Terrace
To market for her dearies,
More mammoth and blowsy with every season;
'Miss Ella's got loony from keeping in cahoots
With eleven cats.'

But now turned kinder with time, we mark Miss Mason
Blinking green-eyed and solitary
At girls who marry –
Demure ones, lithe ones, needing no lesson
That vain jades sulk single down bridal nights,
Accurst as wild-cats.

Sylvia Plath

The Coral Polyp

Let us thank now each polypite
Who laboured with all his tiny might
Through countless aeons till he made us
This little island home, Barbados.

The Spider

I'm told that the spider
Has coiled up inside her
Enough silky material
To spin an aerial
One-way track
to the moon and back;
Whilst I
Cannot even catch a fly.

Turkeys

Christmas tidings of good cheer
To turkeys seldom sound sincere.

The Butterfly

I always think the butterfly
Looks best against a clear blue sky;
I do not think he looks so good
Pinned down within a box of wood.

Frank Collymore

Explanations

Hunting a Hare

jalopy	dilapidated old car
Alpha	first letter of the Greek alphabet
Omega	last letter of the Greek alphabet
frescoes	wall paintings
Dionysus	Greek God of wine

Elephant Song

cicada	a shrill-sounding insect

Ella Mason and Her Eleven Cats

dandies	men very concerned with their appearance
antimacassars	covers for chair-backs
stentorian	loud-voiced
skedaddle	run away
cahoots	company

Some questions on the poems

1. How are the last two and a half lines of *Movements* different from the rest of the poem? In what way are they connected?

2. Madeline Munro in *Milking Time* contrasts her new 'prim, pasteurised' life with her former life on the farm. What exactly does she miss?

3. How did owning so many cats affect Ella Mason's life and character?

4. In *Pig Farm Supreme* Wes Magee stresses the smartness and expensive taste of the 'big house'. What details give this impression? Why do you think he wants to emphasize them?

5. An important element in *Hen Dying* is the character of the poet himself. Can you write a brief description of him?

6. In what way is *The Early Purges* a poem about growing up?

Looking more closely at *Hunting a Hare*

7.
   a) From the first three verses, what mood would you say the writer was in when he and the others set off to hunt the hare?
   b) Where do you think this mood begins to change? What causes the change?
   c) What does Voznesensky suggest can result from man's enthusiasm for killing animals?
   d) In several places in the poem the hare is described as being almost human. Can you quote some examples of this and say what effect the comparisons have on your own feelings for the hare?
   e) What do you think the poet is suggesting when, on the return journey, their faces 'burned like traffic lights'?

Comparisons

1. Several poems touch upon life on a farm. Choose two or three of these and say what different attitudes towards animals are described. What are your own feelings about these attitudes?

2. *Elephant Song* and *Hunting a Hare* are both about hunting, but the feelings they express are quite different. Why? What is the essential difference between the two forms of hunting? Which seems to you to be more justified?

3. Two poems express delight in the movements of animals and birds. Which two? Read them again and discuss their contrasting forms of expression and their qualities as poetry.

Writing a poem

What aspect of man's relationship with animals interests you most? Working with them? Hunting them? Protecting them? Training them? Using them in sport or for entertainment? Keeping them as pets? Admiring them for what they are? Write about what interests you in the form of a poem. Draw upon your own experience with animals as much as you can and/or try to express your feelings about the way animals are treated today.

Possible Futures

Perhaps at no time in human history has there been such a concern about the future as there is today. It is both astonishing and worrying to look back over the last half century at all the changes that have taken place, from the development of nuclear weapons to landing on the moon. At the same time there is a deep and sometimes disturbing fascination about the possibilities that may lie ahead.

The following poems are about the future – perhaps an impossible one, perhaps a real one – who can know? They begin with a honeymoon in space and end with a last message from a world in conflict. In between there are various strange and horrible encounters.

Suggestions for reading the poems

Breakfast in Space	One reader.
Interferences ix	One reader for the commentator; a second reader to do the countdown.
Verdict	A separate reader for each verse.
We'll All Be Spacemen Before We Die	A separate reader for each verse.
Poem Written After Sighting an Unidentified Flying Object	Each verse is complete in itself. There could be a verse each for fourteen readers or two verses for seven readers.
Jeux d'Enfants	A nursery rhyme each for eight readers.
Shoot-out on Little Earth	A verse each for ten readers with a chorus joining in the last two lines of each verse.
Progression of the Species	A separate reader for each verse.
The Basilisk	One reader throughout; or a separate reader for each of the nine verses; or five readers for these verses: 1, 2–4, 5, 6–7, 8–9.
Frankenstein	One reader.
The Gourds	One reader.
Last Message	One reader.

Breakfast in Space

A honeymoon in space. You have
Arrived. Breakfast above

Madagascar, everything mute.
You dine together on passion fruit.

The computer
Has wished you good day. 'A fruit or

Cereal breakfast?' he asked.
You chose. It came flasked

Down a chute. You opened
It with your nuptial friend.

It said 'Open at other end'.
You did. You can depend

On things far more
In space. You go for

A float inside
The fuselage with your bride.

Later you might stride,
Inverted, with giddy pride,

On the exteriority of
The capsule with your love.

Be amicable all day. If
You have your first tiff

Here she might close the door and sever
Your partnership for ever.

She takes away your dish
(The only thing on board British)

To the astrosink;
Before you can think

To thank her
You're over Sri Lanka.

Paul Groves

Interferences   ix

bringing you live
the final preparations
for this great mission
should be coasting
the rings of Saturn
two years time
cloudless sky, and
an unparalleled
world coverage
we have countdown
    ten
may not have told you
    nine
the captain's mascot
    eight
miniaturized gonk
    seven
chief navigator
    six
had twins Tuesday
    five
the Eiffel Tower for
    four
comparison, gantries
    three
aside, so the fuel
    two
huge cloud of
    one
a perfect
    a half
I don't quite
    a quarter
something has clearly
    an eighth
we do not have lift-off
    a sixteenth
we do not have lift-off
    a thirty-second

we do not have lift-off
    a sixty-fourth
we do not have lift-off
    a hundred and twenty-eighth
wo de nat hove loft-iff   *Edwin Morgan*

Verdict

What now with slow and clumsy pride we make –
Space-suit and module, lunar vehicle –
To you, our children, will most surely look
Ridiculous: no Man-made Miracle,
But lonely clutter of some yet-to-be
Museum of Moon Archaeology.

You could see us now, scattering artefacts
In the timeless craters, giving them a past:
Man's mark upon those dreary-pallored crags
In gear abandoned, flag and radar mast –
Top layer in that age-old rubbish heap
Of bones and potsherds, left for you to keep.

You'll mock on archive film the awkward gait
Of our explorers, puppet Michelin Men
Bobbing in moon-walk, slow, grotesquely white,
As though pumped up with too much oxygen,
Who with their slapstick lighten the black sky
Or stoop, papoose backs tilted painfully.

Will you, controllers of undreamed-of skill,
Sophisticated, unencumbered, free
Of our dumb evolution, hard to kill,
Watch us, the stumbling clowns, indulgently?
Pity our innocence? Or turn strange eyes,
O travellers unborn, to untamed skies?   *Jennifer Dines*

We'll All Be Spacemen Before We Die

We'll all be spacemen before we die
    flying in purple ships
            to the sun
  like children
  on their first trip
        to the sea.

We'll all be spacemen before we die
    striding across
           blue meadows
  the rain
    under our feet.

We'll all be spacemen before we die
    sleeping
    between black velvet sheets
    woken
    only by the moon.

Mike Evans

Poem Written After Sighting an Unidentified Flying Object

They are above us,
Beyond us and around us,
Out of space out of time.

Between star and star,
New moons, and beings wiser
Than ourselves, approach.

Our earth is rotten
As a fruit about to drop
Into nothingness.

They are gardeners
Of space, who come to tend us.
Strangers, they love us.

In ages long past
They came to our planet.
We drove them away.

Ever since that day
Our world moves to destruction.
Death grows among us.

Only if we call
To the beautiful strangers
Will our peace return.

I know they watch me
As I write this poem now.
Poets are cosmic.

I feel their silence
Like words, their absence like love.
We must turn to them.

We must watch for them.
We must give our hearts and souls,
Open eyes and arms.

Look to the heavens
And upon the ground for signs.
They are among us.

And we shall see them
With the eyes of vision, if
We have sense to see.

And we shall know them
By their purity and grace,
If we have hearts to feel.

They are above us,
Beyond us and around us,
Out of space out of time.

James Kirkup

Jeux d'Enfants

Hush-a-bye, baby, on the tree top,
When the winds change the fall-out may stop;
When the truce breaks the napalm will fall;
Up will go baby, grannie and all.
Little Bo-Peep has lost her sheep,
And can't tell where to find them;
None will survive, and if she's alive
Her future trails behind them.
Little Boy Blue heard Gabriel's horn;
There's blood in the meadow and fire in the corn.
Where are the boys who followed like sheep?
They're under the haycock, buried deep.
    See-saw, marching to war,
    Neutrons will be our new masters;
    There will be but the Devil to pay
    Because of Atomic Disasters.
        Little Jack Horner
        Flat in a corner
        Under a mushroom sky;
        He bites on his thumb,
        Is sightless and numb
        And praying 'Please God let me die.'
        Little Miss Muffet
        Now has to rough it,
        Eating her heart away;
        With no one beside her,
        Mutation inside her
        Has frightened survivors away.
        'Bye, Baby Bunting,
        Submarines are hunting.
        Please inform our next-of-kin
        We tracked the guided missiles in.
            Ring-a-ring o' roses,
            The final chapter closes.
            I KISS you – I'll MISS you.
                All fall down.

S. Russell Jones

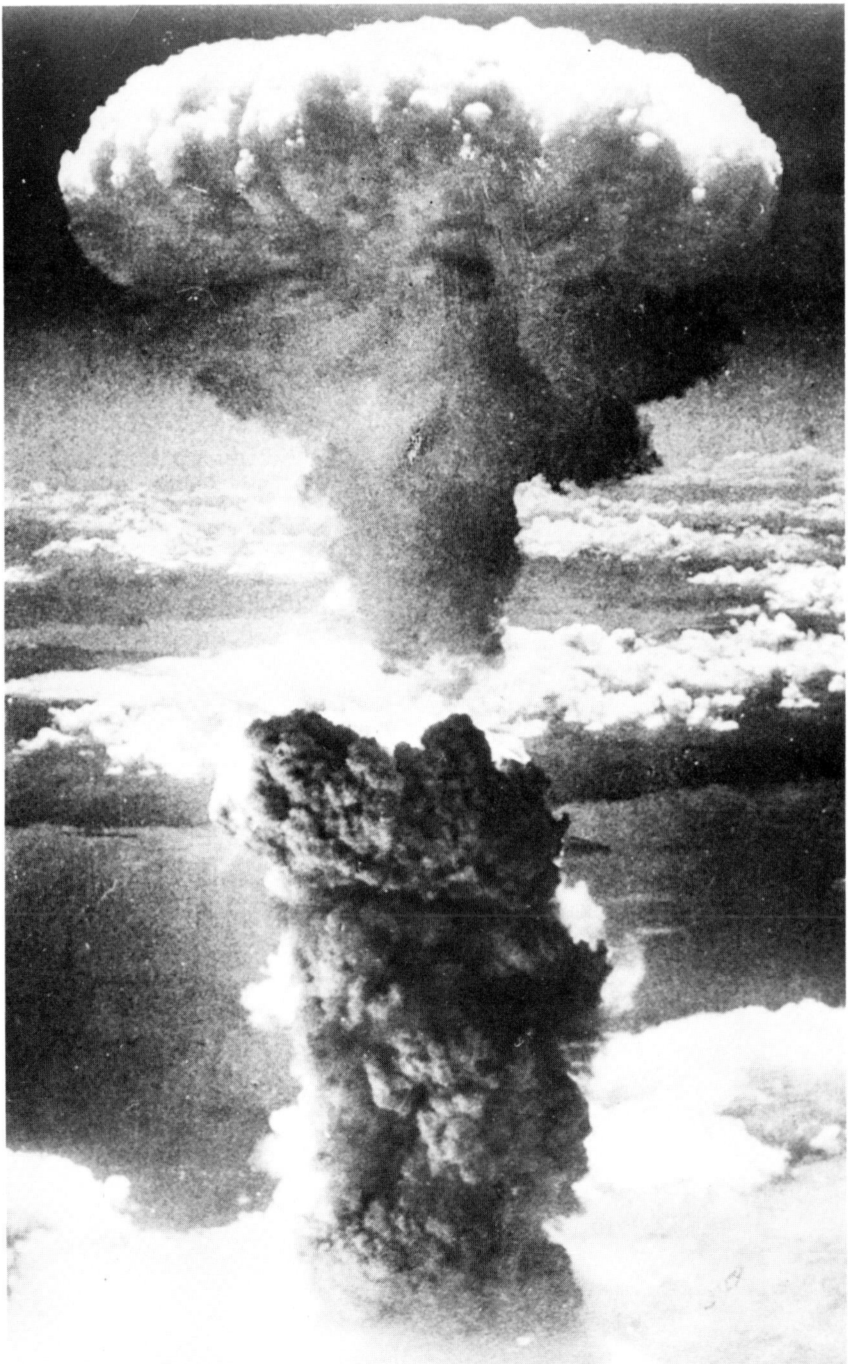

Shoot-out on Little Earth

The president was the meanest sonofabitch
that ever hit the trail
and the president toted a warhead or two
and he reckoned they couldn't fail
– yes sir!
he reckoned they couldn't fail.

Now, the president clinked to one end of the world,
he aimed to maintain the law.
He was the sheriff of the capitalist west
and he was quick on the draw
– doggone!
he was quick on the draw.

Then, Commie the Kid came out the saloon
at the other end of the street.
His missiles was loose in his holster.
It was noon, in the dust and heat
– yep!
it was noon, in the dust and heat.

The president had sworn he'd make first strike
and he guessed he knew its worth,
so he told the Kid to reach for the clouds
at the shoot-out on Little Earth
– gee whiz!
at the shoot-out on Little Earth.

Now, the president was the son of the son of a gun
and was trigger-happy as well,
so half of Asia bit the dust
when he launched his bit of hell
– yippee!
when he launched his bit of hell.

I can tell you the Kid wasn't slow to reply.
His nuclear subs was triggered
and the whole of Europe went up in flames.
It was more or less what he'd figgered
– sure thing!
it was, more or less, what he'd figgered.

Next, the president loosed his projectiles,
each from an underground launching site.
When they hit their pre-planned targets
you couldn't tell day from night
– no sir!
you couldn't tell day from night.

It was empty saddles in the old corral
way down to the Middle East,
and the fall-out lay thick on Africa
and the fire-storms never ceased
– no sir!
the fire-storms never ceased.

But before radiation reached his bones
the Kid had some time on his side
and his pre-aimed rockets found their marks
and the North Americans died
– sure thing!
the North Americans died.

The Pacific Ocean seethed that day,
South America waited for death.
Humanity was headed for the last round-up
that there'd be on Little Earth
– yes sir!
the last on Little Earth.

Bob Dixon

Progression of the Species

Long before a woman knows she's pregnant
And greets the news with fear or smiles
The news has head and heart and heartbeats.
It's then no bigger than a tadpole.
The cells are working on that.
Although I never understood how
A radio set works, this cellular multiplicity
Comes within the realm of graspable ideas
And proves itself pure madness.
Those cells are programmed with the stuttering messages
Called life. Our generation's cracked
The code of life – we know about
The information in the genes inside the chromosomes.

Soon they'll have it all pegged,
Know which nucleic acid brings us curly hair
Which schizophrenic tendencies
Which gift of gab
Which stronger eyesight
Which sweet temper.
Because people are never content with being
Clever, they'll have to get cleverer.
They'll find a way, a century from now,
To make a synthetic gene, a splendid little thing,
To insert it – hypodermic gliding through the testicles –
Into the proto-embryo.

It'll be the end of us and the beginning
Of perfect people
Sweet temper artificially disseminated
A DNA utopia with never an angry word or
Cruel deed. Let's face it though
We hate change. The thought of perfection
Scares us the moment we
Have head and heart and heartbeats.

You know why. Mischief's our common lot –
Original sin is not half as original
As perfection. Those better people
Would look back on us with a loving sorrow
As the Neanderthals of the pre-DNA Age.
In them, the gaudy inferno of the undermind
Would droop and die and disappear
Unregretted – as with us, each generation
The Neanderthal dies from us
Our head and heart and heartbeats.

This is the progression of the species.
We can manage it for ourselves, thanks,
From now on.

Brian W. Aldiss

The Basilisk

Lifting a tangle of roots away from the bank I found
a serpent hatching cocks' eggs; and already the
X-ray blackness of the small basilisks could be
seen moving in the opalescent membranes. I
took up
two in each hand, watched by the torpid serpent.

Back to the
glass-fronted bungalow, laid my a-
mazing discovery on the polished table. Four
active eggs! I
filled a tray with sand and set them on it. They
writhed and
struggled, wrestled with one another through the rubbery
               obstruction. One, the
largest, was almost always on top.

   Night
fell; I drew the Venetian blinds; called for a
lamp. Sat
avidly over the lighted arena.

Darkness
hung at the window; hung behind my head.

Slit
in the glossy rubber: it was the
largest: he
came out hump-necked, butting upward with com-
pacted spines. Small and
blood-red, but faded quickly. A
spruce dragon, 4 inches long; strolled from the eggs' wreckage. I
moved the lamp closer. Had become a
sort of khaki-colour.
                    (History I
thought, like the English army.)
                                    He
walked confidently to the other eggs and
chopped them apart with
long jaws – in a
bloody scramble sucked and chomped, orderlessly
leaping from one to one and in under 85 seconds
was alone with 4 cleaned relics. Had
grown no bigger but was
hard as stone. Stood on the
brink of the tray.

I fitted a bell-jar over his head and
pressured him back to the sand; but a
rap of his front foot
shivered the glass. He
waited impassively under the tumbling shards.

And he be-
gan to grow – was
suddenly 4 feet high, by a-
bout 8 feet long – crouched on the
juddering table. A
massive shadow over the small lamp. I
backed to the door – with a
broom ad-
vanced; whacked at the
solid bulk: somewhere up by the shoulder. As he turned the
lamp crashed
to the floor and smashed. I
fled.

'Come on get out!' In-
sanely I
screamed at the wife and I
hauled the
children, blankets and all, out the back-door. Barricaded the
door of the study. Then from the garage I
dragged two drums of petrol, hacked them gaping
over the barricade, and a
brief fuse
rolled out of newspaper let me escape the catastrophe. The
back-door, left open, created the appropriate draught.

Ex-
plosion! and
fire like a mania. A-
ppalling smashing of glass. Later we discovered the en-
tire house tilted, for in his flight the
basilisk removed the glass-wall's central pillar. E-
laborate damage by fire, and firemen's foam. And
great pits in the garden; of
soil in which we chose not to grow vegetables.

D. M. Black

Frankenstein

I started from my sleep
with horror; a cold dew
covered my forehead,
my teeth chattered,
and every limb became convulsed:
when, by the dim and yellow light
of the moon, as it forced
its way through the window shutters,
I beheld the wretch –
the miserable monster whom I had created.
He held up the curtain of the bed;
and his eyes, if eyes they may be called,
were fixed on me. His jaws opened,
and he muttered some inarticulate sounds,
while a grin wrinkled his cheeks.
He might have spoken,
but I did not hear;
one hand was stretched out,
seemingly to detain me,
but I escaped, and rushed down stairs.
I took refuge in the courtyard
belonging to the house which I inhabited;
where I remained during the rest of the night,
walking up and down in the greatest agitation,
listening attentively,
catching and fearing each sound
as if it were to announce the approach
of the demoniacal corpse
to which I had so miserably given life.

J. R. Colombo

The Gourds

gourd: that's what it was, a gourd. We got in.
We simply scrambled through a gash in its side
and we were in.
Pale yellow it was, very cool and fresh
after the snake swamps.
We had had enough of snakes too –
fifty yards of snake is not for lingering.
But here in the gourd
it was so delicious we made camp,
dried out, rolled a few cigarettes,
opened a tin or two, then slept.
We woke to the sound of our two sentries
being crunched by a sort of Hercules beetle,
too hard for us to attack. We fled
with a handful of stores and clothes out of the gourd
into a gourd about a mile high like
ten Albert Halls – Christ! We
cowered there like so many ticks,
wondering what sort of snakes –
Idly, a vast boa crushed the gourd.
As we spilled out, it was like looking up
into a knot of solid waterspouts, swaying
from the swamp floor to the sky of the dim next gourd.
We floundered, cursing. Something whizzed into my eye.
I fished it out, rubbed the speck between my fingers –
hard, smoothish, slightly ribbed it seemed.
I stared at it, the others – what was left of us –
crowded round. Look, I said. Feel it.
And it felt just like that old

Edwin Morgan

Last Message

The pyramid is closing. Will there be time
for a last message – who can imagine
the grey universe rolling its millions
of last messages as it must do,
unheard, washing everywhere? Oh it is cold
in the pyramid, colder on the plains
where the Forms clash and screech in blue,
our enemies, on their dimensional wheels.
The claws! There were so many dead
the air was hardly to be breathed,
we could neither bury nor burn
in the radiation summer.
Is this our defeat then, as we lock
the white doors, to lie a thousand
thousand thousand years, who knows,
in silence, letting the raucous Forms
go rich and multiply their aquamarine
on ember-red dead dust and men?
Oh those embers, when they raze
every laboratory, pavilion, mast, book,
every chair and hand and lip – blue,
cold, blue, cold, cold
eternity of the embers!
I wish you could hear the wings now
scraping the pyramid, it must be
an unspeakable anger to them
that we few have saved our flesh
and mean to live and think of them
and of the world and of ourselves
and the grey universe that rolls us
a thousand thousand thousand years.

Edwin Morgan

Some questions on the poems

1. *Breakfast in Space* is a light-hearted view of the future. What novelties are in store for honeymooning couples, according to the poem? What things will remain much as they are now?

2. We have all heard of horror movies and horror comics, but we may not have come across a horror poem before. What details in *Frankenstein* would justify calling it a 'horror' poem? Do any other poems in this section come into the same category?

3. How does Edwin Morgan make us feel that the launching of the space mission is taking place *now* in *Interferences* ix? Can you explain the last line of the poem?

4. Describe briefly the catastrophes for mankind that have occurred in *The Gourds* and *Last Message*. Which of these disasters seems to you to be the worse? What do you find effective about the way the poet describes each situation?

5. What qualities does James Kirkup (*Poem Written After Sighting ...*) think the 'beautiful strangers' have and why are they needed on Earth? What leads you to think that the poet intended his readers to take the poem seriously?

6. Can you suggest why S. Russell Jones (*Jeux d'Enfants*) chose to express his vision of nuclear war in the form of nursery rhymes?

7. Do you agree with the poet's opinion in *Verdict*? What is *your* verdict on space exploration so far? What do you think the future holds?

Looking more closely at *Basilisk*

Basilisk: 'Fabulous reptile hatched by serpent from cock's egg, with lethal breath and look.' – *The Concise Oxford Dictionary*

8. a) What is the first hint in the poem that what he (the narrator) found was not quite normal?

b) When he backed to the door, he was obviously feeling threatened by the basilisk. What caused him to be alarmed?
c) The poem reaches a dramatic point when he attempts to blow-up the creature. Can you describe what he did after he had evacuated his wife and children from the bungalow?
d) Check that you are clear about what happened after the explosion, then say why you think the ending either is, or is not, a good one.
e) Why do you think the poem is set out in such a strange way? Sometimes there is only one word to a line and often a word is split between two lines. What effect is the poet aiming at?

Looking more closely at *Progression of the Species*

9
a) What is the 'graspable idea' that Brian Aldiss refers to in the first verse?
b) In the second verse there is a list of characteristics that can be identified as the expression of particular genes. If doctors could implant these genes and produce the characteristics they want, what characteristics do you think parents would choose to have implanted in their future children? What would they avoid?
c) Aldiss says that 'the thought of perfection scares us'. Do you agree? If it were possible to produce 'perfect' human beings, would we go ahead or not?
d) Is the idea behind the poem an impossibility? Or are scientists and doctors moving in that direction already?

Your own writing

1. Three of the poems you have read (including one in 'Speaking Personally') deal with flights through space – all quite extraordinary experiences. Imagine yourself on a flight in the future, travelling alone or with others through the immensity of space. Write a poem about the sensations you experience.

2. As there have been very few 'horror' poems written, perhaps you would like to increase the number by writing one yourself. Take a really frightening situation and give suitably horrific details to your poem.

3. The idea that there are beings 'out there' is a very common one with writers of science fiction and each has his/her own conception of what the extra-terrestrial creatures are like. Examples are James Kirkup's 'beautiful strangers' and Edwin Morgan's 'blue Forms'. Can you produce your own version of this theme in prose or in poetry by imagining a situation in which 'other beings' come to Earth for a very specific reason – with unexpected results?

Index of Poets

Brian W. Aldiss
Progression of the Species — 134

Anonymous
Ballad of Jack Lefroy, The — 64
Banks of the Condamine, The — 66
Bleed'n' Sparrer, The — 90
Elephant Song — 111
Hard Day's Night, A — 88
Jim Jones at Botany Bay — 63
Mailman's Ride, The — 71
Song of the Animal World — 110

James Berry
From Lucy: new generation — 35
Lucy's Letter — 30
Thoughts on my Mother — 32

John Betjeman
Executive — 54

D. M. Black
Basilisk, The — 135

Edward Brathwaite
Ancestors — 24
Emigrants, The — 27

Charles Causley
What Has Happened to Lulu? — 4

Charles Collins
Boiled Beef and Carrots — 87

Frank Collymore
Butterfly, The — 118
Coral Polyp, The — 118
Spider, The — 118
Turkeys — 118

J. R. Colombo
Frankenstein 138

Jennifer Dines
Verdict 127

Bob Dixon
Shoot-out on Little Earth 132

Tommy the Duffle
Teddy Boy 9

Beata Duncan
Commonplace Day, A 45

Ronald Duncan
from *Man* 46

Marriott Edgar
Lion and Albert, The 91
Return of Albert, The 94

Mike Evans
We'll All Be Spacemen Before We Die 128

U. A. Fanthorpe
Family Entertainment 50
Watcher, The 42

Vicki Feaver
Children 3
Latch-key Child 12

Christina Forbes Middleton
Omnibus Edition 97

Zulfikar Ghose
Difficult Child, A 12

Paul Groves
Breakfast in Space 125

Madge Hales
And Not Tears 13

Gerry Hamill
Song of the G.P.O., A   54

Edward Harrington
If Morgan Knew   70

Seamus Heaney
Early Purges, The   115

A. L. Hendriks
Fringe of the Sea, The   26

Cathleen Herbert
Unfold Carefully   42

Helen Hudgell
Into Service   6

Langston Hughes
Mother to Son   5

Evan Jones
Lament of the Banana Man, The   34
Song of the Banana Man, The   21

John Kett
Up Lunnon   90

James Kirkup
Poem Written After Sighting an Unidentified Flying Object   128

Audrey L. Laski
Beauty Queen   9

Edward Lowbury
Doctor Christmas   55

Norman MacCaig
Movements   107
Praise of a Collie   114

Alasdair Maclean
Hen Dying   116

Wes Magee
Pig Farm Supreme   112

Derek Mahon
Bicycle, The   44

Claude McKay
I Shall Return   33

John Mole
Punch Family, The   6

Edwin Morgan
Gourds, The   139
Interferences ix   126
Last Message   140

Mervyn Morris
Letter from England   31

Madeline Munro
Milking Time   113

Richard Murphy
Reading Lesson, The   10

Nicholas Nuttall
Supermarket Tins   8

Will H. Ogilvie
Death of Ben Hall, The   67

Richard Outram
Funambulist   52

A. B. Paterson
Bush Christening, A   76
Mulga Bill's Bicycle   77

Sylvia Plath
Ella Mason and Her Eleven Cats   117
Family Reunion   14

Jimi Rand
Nock Nock Oo Nock E Nock 28

Fred Reed
School Leaver 96

S. Russell Jones
Jeux d'Enfants 130

Peter Thabit Jones
Gower Delivery 41

John Tripp
Night Sorting in Victoria 52
Notes on the Way to the Block 49

W. Tully
Drover's Dream, The 65

Gael Turnbull
How Many Miles 48

Andrei Voznesensky
Hunting a Hare 107

Harry Weston
Knees Up Mother Brown! 85

J. Whitworth
Lovely Morning 3

Frank Wood
Dinner Duty 51

Acknowledgements

The author and publisher are grateful to the following for permission to reproduce poems:

Your Time of Life
Olwyn Hughes Literary Agency for 'Family Reunion' by Sylvia Plath. Martin Secker & Warburg Limited for 'Children' and 'Latch-key Child' from *Close Relatives* by Vicki Feaver and for 'The Punch Family' from *Our Ship* by John Mole. Macmillan, London & Basingstoke for 'A Difficult Child' from *Jets From Orange* by Zulfikar Ghose; David Higham Associates Limited for 'What Has Happened to Lulu?' from *Collected Poems* by Charles Causley; Goldsmith Press, Newbridge, Co. Kildare for 'The Reading Lesson' by Richard Murphy from *Choice*; George Allen & Unwin Ltd. for 'Beauty Queen' by Audrey L. Laski and for 'Teddy Boy' by Tommy the Duffle from *Salome Dear*, John Whitworth for 'Lovely Morning'; Madge Hales for 'And Not Tears'; Random House Inc., USA for 'Mother to Son' by Langston Hughes from *Selected Poems of Langston Hughes*.

Changing Islands
Oxford University Press for 'Ancestors' from *Islands* by Edward Kamau Brathwaite, © Oxford University Press 1969 and for 'The Emigrants' from *Rights of Passage* by Edward Kamau Brathwaite, © Oxford University Press 1967; Harrap Ltd. for 'The Fringe of the Sea' by A. L. Hendriks, 'Nock Nock Oo Nock E Nock' by Jimi Rand, 'Lucy's Letter' and 'From Lucy: new generation' by James Berry from *Bluefoot Traveller* by James Berry; The Estate of Claude McKay for 'I Shall Return' from *The Selected Poems of Claude McKay*.

Speaking Personally
Peter Thabit Jones for 'Gower Delivery'; John Murray Ltd. for 'Executive' by John Betjeman from *The Best of Betjeman*; Oxford University Press for 'The Bicycle' from *Poems 1962–1978* by Derek Mahon, © Derek Mahon 1979; Chatto & Windus Ltd. for 'Funambulist' from *Turns* by Richard Outram; The Ronald Duncan Literary Foundation for Canto 50 from Part IV of 'Man' by Ronald Duncan (1914–1982); John Tripp for 'Notes on the Way to the Block' and 'Night Sorting in Victoria'; Cathleen Herbert for 'Unfold Carefully'; Beata Duncan for 'A Commonplace Day'; Gael Turnbull for his poem 'How Many Miles' from *Rain in Wales* published by Malcolm Rutherford and SATIS; The Statesman & Nation Publishing Co. for 'A Song of the GPO' by Gerry Hamill.

Bush Ballads
Angus & Robertson Publishers and Retusa Pty. Limited for 'Mulga Bill's Bicycle' and 'A Bush Christening' from *The Collected Verse of A. B. Paterson*; Lothian Publishing Company Pty. Ltd. for 'If Morgan Knew' by Edward Harrington from *Boundary Bend and Other Poems*; G.T.A. Ogilvie for 'The Death of Ben Hall' by Will H. Ogilvie.

Countrywide
EMI Music Publishing Ltd. for 'Knees Up Mother Brown!' by Harry Weston © 1939 Peter Maurice Music Co. Ltd., 'The Lion and Albert' by Marriott Edgar © 1933 Francis Day and Hunter Ltd. and for 'The Return of Albert' by Marriott Edgar © 1935 Francis Day and Hunter Ltd.; Christina Forbes Middleton for 'Omnibus Edition' from *Dance of the Village*; John Kett for 'Up Lunnon' from *Tha's a Rum 'un Tew*; Northern House for 'School Leaver' by Fred Reed.

Everything Lives
Macmillan Publishing Co., Inc., USA for 'Elephant Song' and 'Song of the Animal World' from *The Unwritten Song* by Willard R. Trask. Copyright © Willard R. Trask; Victor Gollancz Ltd. for 'Hen Dying' by Alasdair Maclean from *The Wilderness*; Faber & Faber Ltd. for 'The Early Purges' from *Death of a Naturalist* by Seamus Heaney; Olwyn Hughes Literary Agency for 'Ella Mason and Her Eleven Cats' by Sylvia Plath; Madeline Munro for 'Milking Time'; Chatto and Windus Ltd. for 'Movements' by Norman MacCaig from *Measures* and 'Praise of a Collie' by Norman MacCaig from *Tree of Strings*; Basic Books, Inc. for 'Hunting a Hare' by Andrei Voznesensky from *Antiworlds and the Fifth Ace: Poetry by Andrei Voznesensky*, edited by Patricia Blake and Max Hayward. © 1966 by Basic Books, Inc., Publishers. Reprinted by permission of the publisher.

Possible Futures
Carcanet New Press Limited, Manchester for 'The Gourds', 'Last Message' and 'Interferences – ix' from *Poems of Thirty Years* by Edwin Morgan; Jennifer Dines for 'Verdict'; S. Russell Jones for 'Jeux d'Enfants'; Granada Publishing Limited for 'Poem Written After Sighting an Unidentified Flying Object' by James Kirkup from *Frontiers of Going* by John Fairfax; Bob Dixon for 'Shoot-out on Little Earth'.

Despite every effort, the publishers have been unsuccessful in seeking permission to reproduce the following poems. They ask the authors or their agents to contact them about this should this book succeed in coming into their hands: 'Supermarket Tins' by Nicholas Nuttall; 'Into Service' by Helen Hudgell; 'Thoughts on my Mother' by James Berry; 'The Song of the Banana Man' and 'The Lament of the Banana Man' by Evan Jones; 'Letter from England' by Mervyn Morris; 'Doctor

Christmas' by Edward Lowbury; 'Dinner Duty' by Frank Wood; 'The Watcher' and 'Family Entertainment' by U. A. Fanthorpe; 'The Drover's Dream' by W. Tully; 'Pig Farm Supreme' by Wes Magee; 'The Coral Polyp', 'The Spider', 'Turkeys', and 'The Butterfly' by Frank Collymore; 'Breakfast in Space' by Paul Groves; 'We'll All be Spacemen Before We Die' by Mike Evans'; 'Frankenstein' by John Robert Colombo; 'The Basilisk' by D. M. Black; 'Progression of the Species' by Brian W. Aldiss.

Thanks are due to the following for the use of photographs: pp. 1, 22 The J. Allan Cash Photo Library; p. 8 John Topham Picture Library; pp. 11, 19, 39, 47, 50, 63, 86 Barnaby's Picture Library; p. 61 Mary Evans Picture Library; p. 83 Sporting Pictures (UK) Ltd.; p. 92 Methuen Children's Books *The Lion and Albert* by Marriott Edgar, illustrated by Caroline Holden (photographer: George Williams); p. 105 The British Library (India Office Library & Records); p. 113 'Compassion in World Farming', Petersfield, Hants; p. 123 © Lucasfilm Ltd. (LFL) 1983. All rights reserved. COURTESY OF LUCASFILM LTD.; p. 131 Imperial War Museum, London.

It is the express wish of Bob Dixon that no question or other interpretative matter should be set on his poem ('Shoot-out on Little Earth'), whether by schools and other educational establishments or by examining bodies.